D1423904

*T*he Elements of Moral Philosophy

SEVENTH EDITION

JAMES RACHELS

Editions 5–7 by

STUART RACHELS

The McGraw-Hill Companies

Mc Graw Hill
Connect
Learn
Succeed™

THE ELEMENTS OF MORAL PHILOSOPHY, SEVENTH EDITION
International Edition 2012

Exclusive rights by McGraw-Hill Education (Asia), for manufacture and export. This book
cannot be re-exported from the country to which it is sold by McGraw-Hill. This International
Edition is not to be sold or purchased in North America and contains content that is different
from its North American version.

Published by McGraw-Hill, a business unit of The McGraw-Hill Companies, Inc., 1221
Avenue of the Americas, New York, NY 10020. Copyright © 2012 by The McGraw-Hill
Companies, Inc. All rights reserved. Previous editions © 2010, 2007, and 2003. No part of this
publication may be reproduced or distributed in any form or by any means, or stored in a
database or retrieval system, without the prior written consent of The McGraw-Hill
Companies, Inc., including, but not limited to, in any network or other electronic storage or
transmission, or broadcast for distance learning.

Some ancillaries, including electronic and print components, may not be available to
customers outside the United States.

10 09 08 07 06 05 04 03
20 15 14 13
CTP   SLP

All credits appearing on page or at the end of the book are considered to be an extension of
the copyright page.

When ordering this title, use ISBN 978-1-259-00788-0 or MHID 1-259-00788-X

Printed in Singapore

www.mhhe.com

About the Authors

JAMES RACHELS (1941–2003) wrote *The End of Life: Euthanasia and Morality* (1986), *Created from Animals: The Moral Implications of Darwinism* (1990), *Can Ethics Provide Answers? And Other Essays in Moral Philosophy* (1997), *Problems from Philosophy* (first edition, 2005), and *The Legacy of Socrates: Essays in Moral Philosophy* (2007). His website is www.jamesrachels.org.

STUART RACHELS is Associate Professor of Philosophy at the University of Alabama. He has revised several of James Rachels' books, including *Problems from Philosophy* (third edition, 2012) and *The Right Thing to Do* (sixth edition, 2012), which is the companion anthology to this book. Stuart won the United States Chess Championship in 1989, at the age of 20, and today he is a Bronze Life Master at bridge. His website is www.jamesrachels. org/stuart.

Contents

Preface

Socrates, one of the first and best moral philosophers, said that morality is about "no small matter, but how we ought to live." This book is an introduction to moral philosophy, conceived in that broad sense.

In writing this book, I have been guided by the following thought: Suppose that someone has never studied ethics but wants to do so now. What are the first things he or she should learn? This book is my answer to that question. I do not try to cover every topic in the field, nor is my coverage of any particular topic complete. Instead, I try to discuss the ideas that a newcomer should encounter first.

The chapters have been written so that they may be read independently of one another—they are, in effect, separate essays. Thus someone who is interested in Ethical Egoism could go straight to Chapter 5 and find a self-contained introduction to that theory. When read in order, however, the chapters tell a more or less continuous story. The first presents a "minimum conception" of what morality is; the middle chapters cover the most important ethical theories; and the last chapter presents my own view of what a satisfactory moral theory would be like.

The point of this book is not to provide a neat, unified account of "the truth" about ethics. That would be a poor way to introduce the subject. Philosophy is not like physics. In physics, there is a large body of established truth that beginners must patiently master. (Physics teachers rarely invite their students to make up their own minds about the laws of thermodynamics.) There are, of course, unresolved controversies in physics, but these take place against a background of broad agreement. In philosophy, by contrast, everything is controversial—or almost everything. Some of the fundamental issues are still up for grabs. A good introduction will not try to hide that somewhat embarrassing fact.

You will find, then, a survey of contending ideas, theories, and arguments. I find some of these proposals more appealing than others, and a philosopher who made different assessments would no doubt write a different book. Thus, my own views inevitably color the presentation. But I try to present the contending ideas fairly, and when I pass judgment on an argument, I do my best to explain why. Philosophy, like morality itself, is first and last an exercise in reason; we should embrace the ideas that are best supported by the arguments. If this book is successful, then the reader can begin to assess where the weight of reason rests.

About the Seventh Edition

The seventh edition includes no major changes, but many parts of the book have been improved.

- In Chapter 1, "What Is Morality?" I added detail to the claim that our concept of death has changed over the last 50 years (section 1.2).
- In Chapter 2, "The Challenge of Cultural Relativism," I expanded the discussion of monogamy (section 2.9).
- In Chapter 3, "Subjectivism in Ethics," I replaced the Jerry Falwell quote with a Michele Bachmann quote (section 3.1); I corrected some terminology about beliefs and attitudes stemming from Charles L. Stevenson's work (section 3.4); and I expanded our discussion of homosexuality (section 3.7).
- In Chapter 4, "Does Morality Depend on Religion?" I corrected our account of the history of Catholic thought on abortion. In previous editions, we erroneously said that the alleged spotting of "homunculi" under primitive microscopes had a profound effect on the Church's position.
- In Chapter 5, "Ethical Egoism," the Principle of Equal Treatment has been reformulated to say: "We should treat people in the same way unless there is a good reason not to."
- Chapter 6 is now called "The Social Contract Theory" (rather than "The Idea of a Social Contract").
- In Chapter 8, "The Debate over Utilitarianism," I reformulated the account of Classical Utilitarianism that opens the chapter. The new account explains what "equal consideration" is. Also, I now mention the charge that Utilitarianism would support "the tyranny of the majority" in its trampling of individual rights (section 8.3). Finally, the first defense of Utilitarianism has

been renamed "Contesting the Consequences" (from "Denying That the Consequences Would Be Good") (section 8.5).

- At the end of Chapter 10, "Kant and Respect for Persons," I now explain why the debate between retributivists and utilitarians may hinge on the debate over free will.
- Chapter 12 is now called "Virtue Ethics" (rather than "The Ethics of Virtue"). I rewrote the subsection on honesty (section 12.2).

Other changes are too small to mention.

For their help, I thank Keith Augustine, Thomas Avery, Luke Barber, Matthew Brophy, Michael Huemer, Kaave Lajevardi, Sean McAleer, Cayce Moore, Filimon Peonidis, Howard Pospesel, Brian Schimpf, Stephen J. Sullivan, Steve Sverdlik, and McGraw-Hill's outstanding anonymous reviewers. My biggest debts are to my research assistant, Daniel Hollingshead; to my wife, Professor Heather Elliott; and to my mother, Carol Rachels, whose advice again proved enormously helpful.

We all miss James Rachels, who was the sole author of this book in its first four editions. To learn more about him, visit www.jamesrachels.org.

Tell me your thoughts about the book: srachels@bama. ua.edu.

—Stuart Rachels

CHAPTER 1

What Is Morality?

We are discussing no small matter, but how we ought to live.

SOCRATES, IN PLATO'S *REPUBLIC* (ca. 390 B.C.)

1.1. The Problem of Definition

Moral philosophy is the study of what morality is and what it requires of us. As Socrates said, it's about "how we ought to live"—and why. It would be helpful if we could begin with a simple, uncontroversial definition of what morality is, but that turns out to be impossible. There are many rival theories, each expounding a different conception of what it means to live morally, and any definition that goes beyond Socrates's simple formulation is bound to offend at least one of them.

This should make us cautious, but it need not paralyze us. In this chapter, I will describe the "minimum conception" of morality. As the name suggests, the minimum conception is a core that every moral theory should accept, at least as a starting point. First, however, we will examine some moral controversies having to do with handicapped children. Our discussion will bring out the features of the minimum conception.

1.2. First Example: Baby Theresa

Theresa Ann Campo Pearson, an infant known to the public as "Baby Theresa," was born in Florida in 1992. Baby Theresa had anencephaly, one of the worst genetic disorders. Anencephalic infants are sometimes referred to as "babies without brains," but that is not quite accurate. Important parts of the brain—the cerebrum and cerebellum—are missing, as is the top of the skull. The brain stem, however, is still there, and so the baby can still breathe and possess a heartbeat. In the United States,

1

most cases of anencephaly are detected during pregnancy, and the fetuses are usually aborted. Of those not aborted, half are stillborn. About 350 are born alive each year, and they usually die within days.

Baby Theresa's story is remarkable only because her parents made an unusual request. Knowing that their baby would die soon and could never be conscious, Theresa's parents volunteered her organs for immediate transplant. They thought her kidneys, liver, heart, lungs, and eyes should go to other children who could benefit from them. Her physicians agreed. Thousands of infants need transplants each year, and there are never enough organs available. But Theresa's organs were not taken, because Florida law forbids the removal of organs until the donor is dead. By the time Baby Theresa died, nine days later, it was too late—her organs had deteriorated too much to be harvested and transplanted.

Baby Theresa's case was widely debated. Should she have been killed so that her organs could have been used to save other children? A number of professional "ethicists"—people employed by universities, hospitals, and law schools, who get paid to think about such things—were asked by the press to comment. Most of them disagreed with the parents and physicians. Instead, they appealed to time-honored philosophical principles to oppose taking the organs. "It just seems too horrifying to use people as means to other people's ends," said one such expert. Another explained: "It's unethical to kill person A to save person B." And a third added: "What the parents are really asking for is, Kill this dying baby so that its organs may be used for someone else. Well, that's really a horrendous proposition."

Is it horrendous? Opinions were divided. These ethicists thought so, while the parents and doctors did not. But we are interested in more than what people happen to think. We want to know what's true. Were the parents right or wrong to volunteer their baby's organs for transplant? To answer this question, we have to ask what reasons, or arguments, can be given on each side. What can be said to justify the parents' request or to justify opposing their request?

The Benefits Argument. The parents believed that Theresa's organs were doing her no good, because she was not conscious and would die soon anyway. The other children, however, could benefit from them. Thus, the parents seem to have reasoned: *If we can benefit someone without harming anyone else, we ought to do so. Transplanting the organs would benefit the other children without harming Baby Theresa. Therefore, we ought to transplant the organs.*

Is this correct? Not every argument is sound. In addition to knowing what arguments can be given for a view, we also want to know whether those arguments are any good. Generally speaking, an argument is sound if its assumptions are true and the conclusion follows logically from them. In this case, we might wonder about the assertion that Theresa wouldn't be harmed. After all, she would die, and isn't being alive better than being dead? But on reflection, it seems clear that, in these tragic circumstances, the parents were right. Being alive is a benefit only if it enables you to carry on activities and have thoughts, feelings, and relations with other people—in other words, if it enables you to *have a life*. Without such things, biological existence has no value. Therefore, even though Theresa might remain alive for a few more days, it would do her no good.

The Benefits Argument, therefore, provides a powerful reason for transplanting the organs. What arguments exist on the other side?

The Argument That We Should Not Use People as Means. The ethicists who opposed the transplants offered two arguments. The first was based on the idea that *it is wrong to use people as means to other people's ends.* Taking Theresa's organs would be using her to benefit the other children; therefore, it should not be done.

Is this argument sound? The idea that we should not "use" people is obviously appealing, but this is a vague notion that needs to be clarified. What exactly does it mean? "Using people" typically involves violating their *autonomy*—their ability to decide for themselves how to live their own lives, according to their own desires and values. A person's autonomy may be violated through manipulation, trickery, or deceit. For example, I may pretend to be your friend, when I am only interested in going out with your sister; or I may lie to you so you'll give me money; or I may try to convince you that you will enjoy going to the movies, when I only want you to give me a ride. In each case, I am manipulating you in order to get something for myself. Autonomy is also violated when people are forced to do things against their will. This explains why "using people" is wrong; it is wrong because it thwarts people's autonomy.

Taking Baby Theresa's organs, however, could not thwart her autonomy, because she has no autonomy—she cannot make decisions, she has no desires, and she cannot value anything. Would taking her organs be "using her" in any other morally significant sense? We would, of course, be using her organs for someone else's benefit. But we do that every time we perform a transplant. We would also be using her organs without her permission. Would that make it wrong? If we were using them *against* her wishes, then that would be a reason for objecting—it would violate her autonomy. But Baby Theresa has no wishes.

When people are unable to make decisions for themselves, and others must do it for them, there are two reasonable guidelines that might be adopted. First, we might ask, *What would be in their own best interests?* If we apply this standard to Baby Theresa, there would be no objection to taking her organs, for, as we have already noted, her interests will not be affected. She is not conscious, and she will die soon no matter what.

The second guideline appeals to the person's own preferences: We might ask, *If she could tell us what she wants, what would she say?* This sort of thought is useful when we are dealing with people who have preferences (or once had them) but cannot express them—for example, a comatose patient who signed a living will before slipping into the coma. But, sadly, Baby Theresa has no preferences about anything, nor has she ever had any. So we can get no guidance from her, even in our imaginations. The upshot is that we are left to do what we think is best.

The Argument from the Wrongness of Killing. The ethicists also appealed to the principle that *it is wrong to kill one person to save another.* Taking Theresa's organs would be killing her to save others, they said; so, taking the organs would be wrong.

Is this argument sound? The prohibition against killing is certainly among the most important moral rules. Nevertheless, few people believe it is *always* wrong to kill—most people think there are exceptions, such as killing in self-defense. The question, then, is whether taking Baby Theresa's organs should be regarded as an exception to the rule. There are many reasons to think so: Baby Theresa is not conscious; she will never have a life; she is going to die soon; and taking her organs would help the other babies. Anyone who accepts this will regard the argument as flawed. Usually, it is wrong to kill one person to save another, but not always.

There is another possibility. Perhaps we should regard Baby Theresa as already dead. If this sounds crazy, bear in mind that our conception of death has changed over the years. In 1967, the South African doctor Christiaan Barnard performed the first heart transplant in human beings. This was an exciting development; heart transplants could potentially save many lives. It was not clear, however, whether any lives could be saved in the United States. Back then, American law understood death as occurring when the heart stops beating. But once a heart stops beating, it quickly degrades and becomes unsuitable for transplant. Thus, under American law, it was not clear whether any hearts could be legally harvested for transplant. So, American law changed. We now understand death as occurring, not when the heart stops beating, but when the brain stops functioning: "brain death" is our new end-of-life standard. This solved the problem about transplants, because a brain-dead patient can still have a healthy heart, suitable for transplant.

Anencephalics do not meet the technical requirements for brain death as it is currently defined; but perhaps the definition should be revised to include them. After all, they lack any hope for conscious life, because they have no cerebrum or cerebellum. If the definition of brain death were reformulated to include anencephalics, we would become accustomed to the idea that these unfortunate infants are born dead, and so taking their organs would not involve killing them. The Argument from the Wrongness of Killing would then be moot.

On the whole, then, the arguments in favor of transplanting Baby Theresa's organs seem stronger than the arguments against it.

1.3. Second Example: Jodie and Mary

In August 2000, a young woman from Gozo, an island south of Italy, discovered that she was carrying conjoined twins. Knowing that the health-care facilities on Gozo were inadequate to deal with such a birth, she and her husband went to St. Mary's

Hospital in Manchester, England. The infants, known as Mary and Jodie, were joined at the lower abdomen. Their spines were fused, and they had one heart and one pair of lungs between them. Jodie, the stronger one, was providing blood for her sister.

No one knows how many sets of conjoined twins are born each year, but the number has been estimated at 200. Most die shortly after birth, but some do well. They grow to adulthood and marry and have children themselves. But the outlook for Mary and Jodie was grim. The doctors said that without inter-vention the girls would die within six months. The only hope was an operation to separate them. This would save Jodie, but Mary would die immediately.

The parents, who were devout Catholics, refused permis-sion for the operation on the grounds that it would hasten Mary's death. "We believe that nature should take its course," they said. "If it's God's will that both our children should not survive, then so be it." The hospital, hoping to save Jodie, peti-tioned the courts for permission to perform the operation any-way. The courts agreed, and the operation was performed. As expected, Jodie lived and Mary died.

In thinking about this case, we should distinguish the question of *who should make the decision* from the question of *what the decision should be.* You might think, for example, that the decision should be left to the parents, and so the courts should not have intruded. But there remains the separate ques-tion of what would be the wisest choice for the parents (or any-one else) to make. We will focus on that question: Would it be right or wrong to separate the twins?

The Argument That We Should Save as Many as We Can. The rationale for separating the twins is that we have a choice between saving one infant or letting both die. Isn't it plainly better to save one? This argument is so appealing that many people will conclude, without further thought, that the twins should be separated. At the height of the controversy, the *Ladies' Home Journal* commissioned a poll to discover what Americans thought. The poll showed that 78% approved of the operation. People were obviously persuaded by the idea that we should save as many as we can. Jodie and Mary's parents, however, believed that there is an even stronger argument on the other side.

The Argument from the Sanctity of Human Life. The parents loved both of their children, and they thought it would be wrong to kill one of them even to save the other. Of course, they were not alone in thinking this. The idea that all human life is precious, regardless of age, race, social class, or handicap, is at the core of the Western moral tradition. It is especially emphasized in religious writings. In traditional ethics, the prohibition against killing innocent humans is absolute. It does not matter if the killing would serve a good purpose; it simply cannot be done. Mary is an innocent human being, and so she may not be killed.

Is this argument sound? The judges who heard the case did not think so, for a surprising reason. They denied that the operation would kill Mary. Lord Justice Robert Walker said that the operation would merely separate Mary from her sister and then "she would die, not because she was intentionally killed, but because her own body cannot sustain her life." In other words, the operation wouldn't kill her; her body's weakness would. And so, the morality of killing is irrelevant.

The Lord Justice, however, has missed the point. It doesn't matter whether we say that Mary's death is caused by the operation or by her body's own weakness. Either way, she will be dead, and we will knowingly have hastened her death. *That's* the idea behind the traditional prohibition against killing the innocent.

There is, however, a more natural objection to the Argument from the Sanctity of Life. Perhaps it is *not* always wrong to kill innocent human beings. For example, such killings may be right when three conditions are met: (a) the innocent human has no future because she is going to die soon no matter what; (b) the innocent human has no wish to go on living, perhaps because she has no wishes at all; and (c) this killing will save others, who can go on to lead full lives. In these rare circumstances, the killing of the innocent might be justified.

1.4. Third Example: Tracy Latimer

Tracy Latimer, a 12-year-old victim of cerebral palsy, was killed by her father in 1993. Tracy lived with her family on a prairie farm in Saskatchewan, Canada. One Sunday morning while his wife and other children were at church, Robert Latimer put Tracy in the cab of his pickup truck and piped in exhaust fumes until she died. At the time of her death, Tracy weighed less than 40 pounds, and she was described as "functioning at the mental level of a three-month-old baby." Mrs. Latimer said that she was relieved to find Tracy dead when she arrived home and added that she "didn't have the courage" to do it herself.

Robert Latimer was tried for murder, but the judge and jury did not want to treat him harshly. The jury found him guilty of only second-degree murder and recommended that the judge ignore the mandatory 10-year sentence. The judge agreed and sentenced him to one year in prison, followed by a year of confinement to his farm. But the Supreme Court of Canada stepped in and ruled that the mandatory sentence must be imposed. Robert Latimer entered prison in 2001 and was paroled in 2008.

Legal questions aside, did Mr. Latimer do anything wrong? This case involves many of the issues that we saw in the other cases. One argument against Mr. Latimer is that Tracy's life was morally precious, and so he had no right to kill her. In his defense, it may be said that Tracy's condition was so catastrophic that she had no prospects of a "life" in any but a biological sense. Her existence had been reduced to pointless suffering, and so killing her was an act of mercy. Considering those arguments, it appears that Robert Latimer acted defensibly. There were, however, other points made by his critics.

The Argument from the Wrongness of Discriminating against the Handicapped. When Robert Latimer was given a lenient sentence by the trial court, many handicapped people felt insulted. The president of the Saskatoon Voice of People with Disabilities, who has multiple sclerosis, said: "Nobody has the right to decide my life is worth less than yours. That's the bottom line." Tracy was killed because she was handicapped, he said, and that is unconscionable. Handicapped people should be given the same respect and the same rights as everyone else.

What are we to make of this? Discrimination is always a serious matter, because it involves treating some people worse than others, for no good reason. Suppose, for example, that a blind person is refused a job simply because the employer doesn't like the idea of hiring someone who can't see. This is no better than refusing to hire someone because she is Hispanic or Jewish or female. Why is this person being treated differently? Is she less able to do the job? Is she less intelligent or less industrious? Does she deserve the job less? Is she less able to benefit from employment? If there is no good reason to exclude her, then it is arbitrary to do so.

Should we think of the death of Tracy Latimer as a case of discrimination against the handicapped? Robert Latimer argued that Tracy's cerebral palsy was not the issue: "People are saying this is a handicap issue, but they're wrong. This is a torture issue. It was about mutilation and torture for Tracy." Just before her death, Tracy had undergone major surgery on her back, hips, and legs, and more surgery was planned. "With the combination of a feeding tube, rods in her back, the leg cut and flopping around and bedsores," said her father, "how can people say she was a happy little girl?" At the trial, three of Tracy's physicians testified about the difficulty of controlling her pain. Thus, Mr. Latimer denied that Tracy was killed because of her disability; she was killed because she was suffering, and because there was no hope for her.

The Slippery Slope Argument. When the Canadian Supreme Court upheld Robert Latimer's sentence, the director of the Canadian Association of Independent Living Centres said that she was "pleasantly surprised." "It would have really been the slippery slope, and opening the doors to other people to decide who should live and who should die," she said.

Other disability advocates echoed this idea. We may feel sympathy for Robert Latimer, it was said; we may even think that Tracy Latimer is better off dead. However, it is dangerous to think like this. If we accept any sort of mercy killing, we will slide down a "slippery slope," and at the bottom of the slope, all life will be held cheap. Where will we draw the line? If Tracy's life is not worth protecting, what about the lives of other disabled people? What about the elderly, the infirm, and other "useless" members of society? In this context, Hitler's program of "racial purification" is often mentioned, implying that we will end up like the Nazis if we take the first step.

Similar "slippery slope arguments" have been used on other issues. Abortion, in vitro fertilization (IVF), and human cloning have all been opposed because of what they might lead to. Sometimes, in hindsight, it is evident that the worries were unfounded. This has happened with IVF, a technique for creating embryos in the lab. When Louise Brown, the first "test tube baby," was born in 1978, there were dire predictions about what might be in store for her and for society as a whole. But none of those predictions came true, and IVF has become routine. Since Louise Brown's birth, over 100,000 American couples have used IVF to have children.

Without the benefit of hindsight, however, slippery slope arguments are hard to assess. As the old saying has it, "It's tough to make predictions, especially about the future." Reasonable people may disagree about what would happen if mercy killing were allowed in cases like Tracy Latimer's. Those inclined to defend Mr. Latimer may find the dire predictions unrealistic, while those who want to condemn him may insist that the predictions are sensible. This kind of disagreement can be hard to resolve.

It is worth noting, however, that slippery slope arguments are easy to abuse. If you are opposed to something but have no good arguments against it, you can always make up a prediction about what it might lead to; and no matter how implausible your prediction is, no one can prove you wrong. That is why such arguments should be approached with caution.

1.5. Reason and Impartiality

What can we learn from all this about the nature of morality? As a start, we may note two main points: first, moral judgments must be backed by good reasons; and second, morality requires the impartial consideration of each individual's interests.

Moral Reasoning. The cases of Baby Theresa, Jodie and Mary, and Tracy Latimer are liable to arouse strong feelings. Such feelings are often a sign of moral seriousness and may be admired. But they can also get in the way of discovering the truth: When we feel strongly about an issue, it is tempting to assume that we just *know* what the truth is, without even having to consider arguments on the other side. Unfortunately, however, we cannot rely on our feelings, no matter how powerful they may be. Our feelings may be irrational; they may be nothing but the products of prejudice, selfishness, or cultural conditioning. At one time, for example, people's feelings told them that members of other races were inferior and that slavery was God's plan.

Moreover, people's feelings can be very different. In the case of Tracy Latimer, some people feel strongly that her father deserved a long prison term, while others feel equally strongly that he should never have been prosecuted. But both of these feelings cannot be correct.

Thus, if we want to discover the truth, we must let our feelings be guided as much as possible by reason. This is the essence of morality. The morally right thing to do is always the thing best supported by the arguments.

This is not a narrow point about a small range of moral views; it is a general requirement of logic that must be accepted by everyone, regardless of their position on any particular issue. The fundamental point may be stated simply. Suppose someone says that you ought to do such-and-such. You may legitimately ask why you should do it, and if no good reason can be given, you may reject the advice as arbitrary or unfounded.

In this way, moral judgments are different from expressions of personal taste. If someone says, "I like coffee," she does not need to have a reason—she is merely stating a fact about her preferences, and nothing more. There is no such thing as "rationally defending" one's like or dislike of coffee. So long as she is accurately reporting her taste, what she says must be true. On the other hand, if someone says that something is morally wrong, he does need reasons, and if his reasons are legitimate, then other people must acknowledge their force. By the same logic, if he has no good reason for what he says, then he is simply making noise, and we may ignore him.

Of course, not every reason that may be advanced is a good reason. There are bad arguments as well as good ones, and much of the skill of moral thinking consists in discerning the difference. But how do we tell the difference? How do we go about assessing arguments? The examples we have considered point to some answers.

The first thing is to get one's facts straight. Often this is not as easy as it sounds. Sometimes key facts are unknown. Other times, matters are so complex that even the experts disagree. Yet another problem is human prejudice. Often we *want* to believe something because it supports our preconceptions. Those who disapprove of Robert Latimer's action, for example, will want to believe the dire predictions of the Slippery Slope Argument; those who approve of his actions will want to reject them. It is easy to think of other examples: People who do not want to give to charity often say that charities are inefficient and corrupt, even when they have no good evidence for this; and people who dislike homosexuals may say that gay men are all pedophiles, even though very few are. But the facts exist independently of our wishes, and responsible moral thinking begins when we try to see things as they are.

Next, we can bring moral principles into play. In our three examples, a number of principles were involved: that we should not "use" people; that we should not kill one person to save another; that we should do what will benefit the people affected by our actions; that every life is sacred; and that it is wrong to discriminate against the handicapped. Most moral arguments consist of principles being applied to particular cases, and so we must ask whether the principles are justified and whether they are being applied correctly.

It would be nice if there were a simple recipe for constructing good arguments and avoiding bad ones. Unfortunately, there is not. Arguments can go wrong in many ways, and we must always be alert to the possibility of new complications and new kinds of error. But that is not surprising. The rote application of routine methods is never a satisfactory substitute for critical thinking, in any area. Morality is no exception.

The Requirement of Impartiality. Almost every important moral theory includes the idea of impartiality. This is the idea that each individual's interests are equally important; no one should get special treatment. At the same time, impartiality requires that we not treat the members of particular *groups* as inferior, and thus it condemns forms of discrimination like sexism and racism.

Impartiality is closely connected with the idea that moral judgments must be backed by good reasons. Consider the racist who thinks that white people deserve all the good jobs. He would like all the doctors, lawyers, business executives, and so on, to be white. Now we can ask for reasons; we can ask why this is thought to be right. Is there something about white people that makes them better fitted for the highest-paying and most prestigious positions? Are they inherently brighter or more industrious? Do they care more about themselves and their families? Would they benefit more from such employment? In each case, the answer is no; and if there is no good reason for treating people differently, then discrimination is unacceptably arbitrary.

The requirement of impartiality, then, is at bottom nothing more than a rule against treating people arbitrarily. It forbids treating one person worse than another when there is no good reason to do so. But if this explains what is wrong with racism, it also explains why, in some cases, it is *not* racist to treat people differently. Suppose a movie director were making a film about Fred Shuttlesworth (1922–2011), the heroic African-American civil rights leader. This director would have a good reason not to cast Christian Bale in the starring role. Such "discrimination" would not be arbitrary or objectionable.

1.6. The Minimum Conception of Morality

We may now state the minimum conception: Morality is, at the very least, the effort to guide one's conduct by reason—that is, to do what there are the best reasons for doing—while giving equal weight to the interests of each individual affected by one's decision.

This gives us a picture of what it means to be a conscientious moral agent. The conscientious moral agent is someone who is concerned impartially with the interests of everyone affected by what he or she does; who carefully sifts facts and examines their implications; who accepts principles of conduct only after scrutinizing them to make sure they are justified; who is willing to "listen to reason" even when it means revising prior convictions; and who, finally, is willing to act on the results of this deliberation.

As one might expect, not every ethical theory accepts this "minimum." This picture of the moral agent has been disputed in various ways. However, theories that reject the minimum conception encounter serious difficulties. Most philosophers realize this, and so most theories of morality incorporate the minimum conception, in one form or another.

CHAPTER 2

The Challenge of Cultural Relativism

Morality differs in every society, and is a convenient term for
socially approved habits.

RUTH BENEDICT, *PATTERNS OF CULTURE* (1934)

2.1. Different Cultures Have Different Moral Codes

Darius, a king of ancient Persia, was intrigued by the variety of
cultures he met in his travels. He had found, for example, that
the Callatians, who lived in India, ate the bodies of their dead
fathers. The Greeks, of course, did not do that—the Greeks
practiced cremation and regarded the funeral pyre as the
natural and fitting way to dispose of the dead. Darius thought
that a sophisticated outlook should appreciate the differences
between cultures. One day, to teach this lesson, he summoned
some Greeks who happened to be at his court and asked what
it would take for them to eat the bodies of their dead fathers.
They were shocked, as Darius knew they would be, and replied
that no amount of money could persuade them to do such a
thing. Then Darius called in some Callatians and, while the
Greeks listened, asked them what it would take for them to
burn their dead fathers' bodies. The Callatians were horrified
and told Darius not to speak of such things.

This story, recounted by Herodotus in his *History*, illustrates a recurring theme in the literature of social science:
Different cultures have different moral codes. What is thought
right within one group may horrify the members of another
group, and vice versa. Should we eat the bodies of the dead

or burn them? If you were a Greek, one answer would seem obviously correct; but if you were a Callatian, the other answer would seem equally certain.

There are many examples of this. Consider the Eskimos of the early and mid-20th century. The Eskimos are the native people of Alaska, northern Canada, Greenland, and northeastern Siberia, in Asiatic Russia. Today, none of these groups call themselves "Eskimos," but the term has historically referred to that scattered Arctic population. Prior to the 20th century, the outside world knew little about them. Then explorers began to bring back strange tales.

The Eskimos lived in small settlements, separated by great distances, and their customs turned out to be very different from ours. The men often had more than one wife, and they would share their wives with guests, lending them out for the night as a sign of hospitality. Moreover, within a community, a dominant male might demand—and get—regular sexual access to other men's wives. The women, however, were free to break these arrangements simply by leaving their husbands and taking up with new partners—free, that is, so long as their former husbands chose not to make too much trouble. All in all, the Eskimo custom of marriage was a volatile practice that bore little resemblance to our custom.

But it was not only their marriages and sexual practices that were different. The Eskimos also seemed to care less about human life. Infanticide, for example, was common. Knud Rasmussen, an early explorer, reported meeting one woman who had borne 20 children but had killed 10 of them at birth. Female babies, he found, were especially likely to be killed, and this was permitted at the parents' discretion, with no social stigma attached. Moreover, when elderly family members became too feeble, they were left out in the snow to die. In Eskimo society, there seemed to be remarkably little respect for life.

Most of us would find these Eskimo customs completely unacceptable. Our own way of living seems so natural and right to us that we can hardly conceive of people who live so differently. When we hear of such people, we might want to say that they're "backward" or "primitive." But to anthropologists, the Eskimos did not seem unusual. Since the time of Herodotus, enlightened observers have known that conceptions of right and wrong differ from culture to culture. If we assume that our ethical ideas will be shared by all cultures, we are merely being naïve.

2.2. Cultural Relativism

To many people, this observation—"Different cultures have different moral codes"—seems like the key to understanding morality. There are no universal moral truths, they say; the customs of different societies are all that exist. To call a custom "correct" or "incorrect" would imply that we can judge that custom by some independent standard of right and wrong. But no such standard exists; every standard is culture-bound. The sociologist William Graham Sumner (1840–1910) put it like this:

> The "right" way is the way which the ancestors used and which has been handed down. . . . The notion of right is in the folkways. It is not outside of them, of independent origin, and brought to test them. In the folkways, whatever is, is right. This is because they are traditional, and therefore contain in themselves the authority of the ancestral ghosts. When we come to the folkways we are at the end of our analysis.

This line of thought, more than any other, has persuaded people to be skeptical about ethics. Cultural Relativism says, in effect, that there is no such thing as universal truth in ethics; there are only the various cultural codes, and nothing more. Cultural Relativism challenges our belief in the objectivity and universality of moral truth.

The following claims have all been made by cultural relativists:

1. Different societies have different moral codes.
2. The moral code of a society determines what is right within that society; that is, if the moral code of a society says that a certain action is right, then that action *is* right, at least within that society.
3. There is no objective standard that can be used to judge one society's code as better than another's. There are no moral truths that hold for all people at all times.
4. The moral code of our own society has no special status; it is but one among many.
5. It is arrogant for us to judge other cultures. We should always be tolerant of them.

These five propositions may seem to go together, but they are *independent* of one another, meaning that some of them may be true even while others are false. Indeed, two of the propositions appear to be inconsistent with each other. The second says that right and wrong are determined by the norms of a society; the fifth says that one should always be tolerant of other cultures. But what if the norms of one's society favor intolerance? For example, when the Nazi army invaded Poland on September 1, 1939, thus beginning World War II, this was an intolerant action of the first order. But what if it conformed to Nazi ideals? A cultural relativist, it seems, cannot criticize the Nazis for being intolerant, if all they're doing is following their own moral code.

Given that cultural relativists take pride in their tolerance, it would be ironic if their theory actually supported the intolerance of warlike societies. However, their theory need not do that. Properly understood, Cultural Relativism holds that the norms of a culture reign supreme *within the bounds of the culture itself.* Thus, once the German soldiers entered Poland, they became bound by the norms of Polish society—norms that obviously excluded the mass slaughter of innocent Poles. "When in Rome," the old saying goes, "do as the Romans do." Cultural relativists agree.

2.3. The Cultural Differences Argument

Cultural Relativists often employ a certain *form of argument.* They begin with facts about cultures and end up drawing a conclusion about morality. Thus, they invite us to accept this reasoning:

(1) The Greeks believed it was wrong to eat the dead, whereas the Callatians believed it was right to eat the dead.

(2) Therefore, eating the dead is neither objectively right nor objectively wrong. It is merely a matter of opinion, which varies from culture to culture.

Or:

(1) The Eskimos saw nothing wrong with infanticide, whereas Americans believe infanticide is immoral.

  (2) Therefore, infanticide is neither objectively right nor objectively wrong. It is merely a matter of opinion, which varies from culture to culture.

Clearly, these arguments are variations of one fundamental idea. They are both examples of a more general argument, which says:

  (1) Different cultures have different moral codes.

  (2) Therefore, there is no objective truth in morality. Right and wrong are only matters of opinion, and opinions vary from culture to culture.

We may call this the Cultural Differences Argument. To many people, it is persuasive. But is it a good argument—is it *sound?*

It is not. For an argument to be sound, its premises must all be true, and the conclusion must follow logically from them. Here, the problem is that the conclusion does not *follow from* the premise—that is, even if the premise is true, the conclusion might still be false. The premise concerns what people *believe*— in some societies, people believe one thing; in other societies, people believe something else. The conclusion, however, concerns what *really is the case.* This sort of conclusion does not follow logically from that sort of premise. In philosophical terminology, this means that the argument is *invalid.*

Consider again the example of the Greeks and Callatians. The Greeks believed it was wrong to eat the dead; the Callatians believed it was right. Does it follow, *from the mere fact that they disagreed*, that there is no objective truth in the matter? No, it does not follow; it could be that the practice was objectively right (or wrong) and that one of them was simply mistaken.

To make the point clearer, consider a different matter. In some societies, people believe the earth is flat. In other societies, such as our own, people believe that the earth is a sphere. Does it follow, from the mere fact that people disagree, that there is no "objective truth" in geography? Of course not; we would never draw such a conclusion, because we realize that the members of some societies might simply be wrong. There is no reason to think that if the world is round, everyone must know it. Similarly, there is no reason to think that if there is moral truth, everyone must know it. The Cultural Differences Argument tries to derive a substantive conclusion about a subject from the mere fact that people disagree. But this is impossible.

This point should not be misunderstood. We are not saying that the conclusion of the argument is false; for all we have said, Cultural Relativism could still be true. The point is that the conclusion does not follow from the premise. This means that the Cultural Differences Argument is invalid. Thus, the argument fails.

2.4. What Follows from Cultural Relativism

Even if the Cultural Differences Argument is unsound, Cultural Relativism might still be true. What would follow if it were true?

In the passage quoted earlier, William Graham Sumner states the essence of Cultural Relativism. He says that the only measure of right and wrong is the standards of one's society: "The notion of right is in the folkways. It is not outside of them, of independent origin, and brought to test them. In the folkways, whatever is, is right." Suppose we took this seriously. What would be some of the consequences?

1. *We could no longer say that the customs of other societies are morally inferior to our own.* This, of course, is one of the main points stressed by Cultural Relativism. We should never condemn a society merely because it is "different." This attitude seems enlightened, so long as we concentrate on examples like the funerary practices of the Greeks and Callatians.

However, we would also be barred from criticizing other, less benign practices. For example, the Chinese government has a long history of repressing political dissent within its own borders. At any given time, thousands of political prisoners in China are doing hard labor, and in the Tiananmen Square episode of 1989, Chinese troops slaughtered hundreds, if not thousands, of peaceful protesters. Cultural Relativism would preclude us from saying that the Chinese government's policies of oppression are wrong. We could not even say that a society that respects free speech is *better* than Chinese society, for that would also imply a universal standard of comparison. The failure to condemn *these* practices does not seem enlightened; on the contrary, political oppression seems wrong wherever it occurs. Nevertheless, if we accept Cultural Relativism, we have to regard such practices as immune from criticism.

2. *We could no longer criticize the code of our own society.* Cultural Relativism suggests a simple test for determining what is right and what is wrong: All we need to do is ask whether the action is in line with the code of the society in question. Suppose a resident of India wonders whether her country's caste system—a system of rigid social hierarchy—is morally correct. All she has to do is ask whether this system conforms to her society's moral code. If it does, there is nothing to worry about, at least from a moral point of view.

This implication of Cultural Relativism is disturbing because few of us think that our society's code is perfect—we can think of ways in which it might be improved. Moreover, we can think of ways in which we might learn from other cultures. Yet Cultural Relativism stops us from criticizing our own society's code, and it bars us from seeing ways in which other cultures might be better. After all, if right and wrong are relative to culture, this must be true for our own culture, just as it is for all other cultures.

3. *The idea of moral progress is called into doubt.* We think that at least some social changes are for the better. Throughout most of Western history, the place of women in society was narrowly defined. Women could not own property; they could not vote or hold political office; and they were under the almost absolute control of their husbands or fathers. Recently, much of this has changed, and most people think of it as progress.

But if Cultural Relativism is correct, can we legitimately view this as progress? Progress means replacing the old ways with new and improved ways. But by what standard do we judge the new ways as better? If the old ways conformed to the standards of *their* time, then Cultural Relativism would not judge them by *our* standards. Sexist 19th-century society was a different society from the one we now inhabit. To say that we have made progress implies that present-day society is better—just the sort of transcultural judgment that Cultural Relativism forbids.

Our ideas about social *reform* will also have to be reconsidered. Reformers such as Martin Luther King Jr. have sought to change their societies for the better. But according to Cultural Relativism, there is only one way to improve a society: to make it better match its own ideals. After all, the society's ideals are the standard by which reform is assessed. No one, however, may

challenge the ideals themselves, for they are by definition correct. According to Cultural Relativism, then, the idea of social
reform makes sense only in this limited way.

These three consequences of Cultural Relativism have led
many people to reject it. Slavery, we want to say, is wrong wherever it occurs, and one's own society can make fundamental
moral progress. Because Cultural Relativism implies that these
judgments make no sense, it cannot be right.

2.5. Why There Is Less Disagreement Than It Seems

Cultural Relativism starts by observing that cultures differ dramatically in their views of right and wrong. But how much do
they really differ? It is true that there are differences, but it is
easy to exaggerate them. Often, what seemed at first to be a big
difference turns out to be no difference at all.

Consider a culture in which people believe it is wrong to
eat cows. This may even be a poor culture, in which there is not
enough food; still, the cows are not to be touched. Such a society would appear to have values very different from our own.
But does it? We have not yet asked *why* these people won't eat
cows. Suppose they believe that after death the souls of humans
inhabit the bodies of animals, especially cows, so that a cow may
be someone's grandmother. Shall we say that their values differ
from ours? No; the difference lies elsewhere. The difference is
in our belief systems, not in our value systems. We agree that
we shouldn't eat Grandma; we disagree about whether the cow
could be Grandma.

The point is that many factors work together to produce
the customs of a society. Not only are the society's values important, but so are its religious beliefs, its factual beliefs, and its
physical environment. Thus, we cannot conclude that two societies differ in value just because they differ in custom. After
all, customs may vary for a number of different reasons. Thus,
there may be less moral disagreement than there appears to be.

Consider again the Eskimos, who killed perfectly healthy
infants, especially girls. We do not approve of such things; in
our society, a parent who kills a baby will be locked up. Thus,
there appears to be a great difference in the values of our two
cultures. But suppose we ask why the Eskimos did this. The

explanation is not that they lacked respect for human life or did not love their children. An Eskimo family would always protect its babies if conditions permitted. But the Eskimos lived in a harsh environment, where food was scarce. To quote an old Eskimo saying: "Life is hard, and the margin of safety small." A family may want to nourish its babies but be unable to do so.

As in many traditional societies, Eskimo mothers would nurse their infants over a much longer period than mothers in our culture—for four years, and perhaps even longer. So, even in the best of times, one mother could sustain very few children. Moreover, the Eskimos were nomadic; unable to farm in the harsh northern climate, they had to keep moving to find food. Infants had to be carried, and a mother could carry only one baby in her parka as she traveled and went about her outdoor work. Finally, the Eskimos lacked birth control, so unwanted pregnancies were common.

Infant girls were more readily killed for two reasons. First, in Eskimo society, the males were the primary food providers—they were the hunters—and food was scarce. Males were thus more valuable to the community. Second, the hunters suffered a high casualty rate, so the men who died prematurely far outnumbered the women who died young. If male and female infants had survived in equal numbers, then the female adult population would have greatly outnumbered the male adult population. Examining the available statistics, one writer concluded that "were it not for female infanticide . . . there would be approximately one-and-a-half times as many females in the average Eskimo local group as there are food-producing males."

Thus, Eskimo infanticide was not due to a fundamental disregard for children. Instead, it arose from the recognition that drastic measures were needed to ensure the group's survival. Even then, however, killing the baby would not be the first option considered. Adoption was common; childless couples were especially happy to take a fertile couple's "surplus." Killing was the last resort. I emphasize this in order to show that the raw data of anthropology can be misleading; it can make the differences in values between cultures seem greater than they are. The Eskimos' values were not all that different from our own. It is only that life forced choices upon them that we do not have to make.

2.6. Some Values Are Shared by All Cultures

It should not surprise us that the Eskimos were protective of their children. How could they not be? Babies are helpless and cannot survive without extensive care. If a group did not protect its young, the young would not survive, and the older members of the group would not be replaced. Eventually the group would die out. This means that any culture that continues to exist must care for its young. Neglected infants must be the exception, not the rule.

Similar reasoning shows that other values must be more or less universal across human societies. Imagine what it would be like for a society to place no value on truth telling. When one person spoke to another, there would be no presumption that she was telling the truth, for she could just as easily be lying. Within that society, there would be no reason to pay attention to what anyone says. If I want to know what time it is, why should I bother asking anyone, if lying is commonplace? Communication would be extremely difficult, if not impossible, in such a society. And because societies cannot exist without communication among their members, society would become impossible. It follows that every society must value truthfulness. There may, of course, be situations in which lying is thought to be okay, but the society will still value honesty in most situations.

Consider another example. Could a society exist in which there was no prohibition against murder? What would this be like? Suppose people were free to kill one another at will, and no one disapproved. In such a "society," no one could feel safe. Everyone would have to be constantly on guard, and everyone would try to avoid other people—those potential murderers— as much as possible. This would result in individuals trying to become self-sufficient. Society on any large scale would thus collapse. Of course, people might band together in smaller groups where they could feel safe. But notice what this means: They would be forming smaller societies that did acknowledge a rule against murder. The prohibition against murder, then, is a necessary feature of society.

There is a general point here, namely, that *there are some moral rules that all societies must embrace, because those rules are necessary for society to exist.* The rules against lying and murder are two examples. And, in fact, we do find these rules in force in all cultures. Cultures may differ in what they regard as legitimate exceptions to the rules, but this disagreement exists against a broad background of agreement. Therefore, we shouldn't over-estimate the extent to which cultures differ. Not every moral rule can vary from society to society.

2.7. Judging a Cultural Practice to Be Undesirable

In 1996, a 17-year-old named Fauziya Kassindja arrived at Newark International Airport in New Jersey and asked for asylum. She had fled her native country of Togo, in West Africa, to escape what people there call "excision." Excision is a permanently disfiguring procedure. It is sometimes called "female circumcision," but it bears little resemblance to male circumcision. In the Western media, it is often referred to as "female genital mutilation."

According to the World Health Organization, excision is practiced in 28 African nations, and about 135 million females have been painfully excised. Sometimes, excision is part of an elaborate tribal ritual performed in small villages, and girls look forward to it as their entry into the adult world. Other times, the practice is carried out in cities on young women who desperately resist.

Fauziya Kassindja was the youngest of five daughters. Her father, who owned a successful trucking business, was opposed to excision, and he was able to defy the tradition because of his wealth. Thus, his first four daughters were married with-out being mutilated. But when Fauziya was 16, he suddenly died. Fauziya then came under the authority of her aunt, who arranged a marriage for her and prepared to have her excised. Fauziya was terrified, and her mother and oldest sister helped her escape.

In America, Fauziya was imprisoned for nearly 18 months while the authorities decided what to do with her. During this time, she was subjected to humiliating strip searches, denied medical treatment for her asthma, and generally treated like a criminal. Finally, she was granted asylum, but not before her case aroused a great controversy. The controversy was not about her treatment in America, but about how we should regard the customs of other cultures. A series of articles in *The New York*

Times encouraged the idea that excision is barbaric and should be condemned. Other observers were reluctant to be so judgmental. Live and let live, they said; after all, our culture probably seems just as strange to outsiders.

Suppose we say that excision is wrong. Are we merely imposing the standards of our own culture? If Cultural Relativism is correct, that is all we can do, for there is no culture-independent moral standard to appeal to. But is that true?

Is There a Culture-Independent Standard of Right and Wrong?

Excision is bad in many ways. It is painful and results in the permanent loss of sexual pleasure. Its short-term effects can include hemorrhage, tetanus, and septicemia. Sometimes it causes death. Its long-term effects can include chronic infection, scars that hinder walking, and continuing pain.

Why, then, has it become a widespread social practice? It is not easy to say. The practice has no obvious social benefits. Unlike Eskimo infanticide, it is not necessary for group survival. Nor is it a matter of religion. Excision is practiced by groups from various religions, including Islam and Christianity.

Nevertheless, a number of arguments are made in its defense. Women who are incapable of sexual pleasure are less likely to be promiscuous; thus, there will be fewer unwanted pregnancies in unmarried women. Moreover, wives for whom sex is only a duty are less likely to cheat on their husbands; and because they are not thinking about sex, they will be more attentive to the needs of their husbands and children. Husbands, for their part, are said to enjoy sex more with wives who have been excised. Unexcised women, the men feel, are unclean and immature.

It would be easy, and perhaps a bit arrogant, to ridicule these arguments. But notice an important feature of them: They try to justify excision by showing that excision is beneficial— men, women, and their families are said to be better off when women are excised. Thus, we might approach the issue by asking whether excision, on the whole, is helpful or harmful.

This points to a standard that might reasonably be used in thinking about any social practice: *Does the practice promote or hinder the welfare of the people affected by it?* But this looks like the sort of independent moral standard that Cultural Relativism forbids. It is a single standard that may be brought to bear in judging the practices of any culture, at any time, including our own. Of course, people will not usually see this principle as being "brought in from the outside" to judge them, because all cultures value human happiness.

Why, Despite All This, Thoughtful People May Be Reluctant to Criticize Other Cultures. Many people who are horrified by excision are nevertheless reluctant to condemn it, for three reasons. First, there is an understandable nervousness about interfering in the social customs of other peoples. Europeans and their descendants in America have a shameful history of destroying native cultures in the name of Christianity and enlightenment. Because of this, some people refuse to criticize other cultures, especially cultures that resemble those that were wronged in the past. There is a difference, however, between (a) judging a cultural practice to be deficient and (b) thinking that we should announce that fact, apply diplomatic pressure, and send in the troops. The first is just a matter of trying to see the world clearly, from a moral point of view. The second is something else entirely. Sometimes it may be right to "do something about it," but often it will not be.

Second, people may feel, rightly enough, that we should be tolerant of other cultures. Tolerance is, no doubt, a virtue—a tolerant person can live in peace with those who see things differently. But nothing about tolerance requires us to say that all beliefs, all religions, and all social practices are equally admirable. On the contrary, if we did not think that some things were better than others, then there would be nothing for us to tolerate.

Finally, people may be reluctant to judge because they do not want to express contempt for the society being criticized. But again, this is misguided: To condemn a particular practice is not to say that the culture on the whole is contemptible. After all, the culture could still have many admirable features. Indeed, we should expect this to be true of most human societies—they are mixtures of good and bad practices. Excision happens to be one of the bad ones.

2.8. Back to the Five Claims

Let us now return to the five tenets of Cultural Relativism that were listed earlier. How have they fared in our discussion?

1. Different societies have different moral codes.

This is certainly true, although there are some values that all cultures share, such as the value of truth telling, the importance of caring for the young, and the prohibition against murder. Also, when customs differ, the underlying reason will often have more to do with the factual beliefs of the cultures than with their values.

2. The moral code of a society determines what is right within that society; that is, if the moral code of a society says that a certain action is right, then that action *is* right, at least within that society.

Here we must bear in mind the difference between what a society *believes* about morals and what is *really true*. The moral code of a society is closely tied to what people in that society believe to be right. However, that code, and those people, can be in error. Earlier, we considered the example of excision— a barbaric practice endorsed by many societies. Consider three more examples, all of which involve the mistreatment of women:

- In 2002, an unwed mother in Nigeria was sentenced to be stoned to death for having had sex out of wedlock. It is unclear whether Nigerian values, on the whole, approved of this verdict, given that it was later overturned by a higher court. However, it was overturned partly to appease the international community. When the Nigerians themselves heard the verdict being read out in the courtroom, the crowd shouted out their approval.
- In 2005, a woman from Australia was convicted of trying to smuggle nine pounds of marijuana into Indonesia. For that crime, she was sentenced to 20 years in prison— an excessive punishment. Under Indonesian law, she might even have received a death sentence.
- In 2007, a woman was gang-raped in Saudi Arabia. When she complained to the police, the police discovered in the course of their investigation that she had recently been alone with a man she was not related to. For that crime, she was sentenced to 90 lashes. When she appealed her conviction, this angered the judges, and they increased

her sentence to 200 lashes plus a six-month prison term. Eventually, the Saudi king pardoned her, although he said he supported the sentence she had received.

Cultural Relativism holds, in effect, that societies are morally infallible—in other words, that the morals of a culture can never be wrong. But when we see that societies can and do endorse grave injustices, we see that societies, like their members, can be in need of moral improvement.

3. There is no objective standard that can be used to judge one society's code as better than another's. There are no moral truths that hold for all people at all times.

It is difficult to think of ethical principles that hold for all people at all times. However, if we are to criticize the practice of slavery, or stoning, or genital mutilation, and if such practices are really and truly wrong, then we must appeal to principles that are not tethered to any particular society. Earlier I suggested one such principle: that it always matters whether a practice promotes or hinders the welfare of the people affected by it.

4. The moral code of our own society has no special status; it is but one among many.

It is true that the moral code of our society has no special status. After all, our society has no heavenly halo around its borders; our values do not have any special standing just because they happen to be ours. However, to say that the moral code of one's own society "is merely one among many" seems to imply that all codes are the same—that they are all more or less equally good. In fact, it is an open question whether a given code "is merely one among many." That code might be among the best; it might be among the worst.

5. It is arrogant for us to judge other cultures. We should always be tolerant of them.

There is much truth in this, but the point is overstated. We *are* often arrogant when we criticize other cultures, and tolerance *is* generally a good thing. However, we shouldn't tolerate everything. Human societies have done terrible things, and it is a mark of progress when we can say that those things are in the past.

2.9. What We Can Learn from Cultural Relativism

So far, in discussing Cultural Relativism, I have dwelt mostly on its shortcomings. I have said that it rests on an unsound argument, that it has implausible consequences, and that it suggests greater moral disagreement than exists. This all adds up to a rejection of the theory. Nevertheless, you may have the feeling that this is a little unfair. The theory must have something going for it—why else has it been so influential? In fact, I think there is something right about Cultural Relativism, and there are two lessons we should learn from it.

First, Cultural Relativism warns us, quite rightly, about the danger of assuming that all of our practices are based on some absolute rational standard. They are not. Some of our customs are merely conventional—merely peculiar to our society—and it is easy to lose sight of that fact. In reminding us of this, the theory does us a service.

Funerary practices are one example. The Callatians, according to Herodotus, were "men who eat their fathers"—a shocking idea, to us at least. But eating the flesh of the dead could be understood as a sign of respect. It could be seen as a symbolic act which says, "We wish this person's spirit to dwell within us." Perhaps this is how the Callatians saw it. On this way of thinking, burying the dead could be seen as an act of rejection, and burning the corpse as positively scornful. Of course, the idea of eating human flesh may repel us, but so what? Our revulsion may be only a reflection of our society. Cultural Relativism begins with the insight that many of our practices are like this—they are only cultural products. Then it goes wrong by inferring that, because some practices are like this, all of them must be.

Or consider modesty of dress. In America, a woman is not supposed to display her breasts in public. For example, during the 2004 Super Bowl halftime show, Justin Timberlake ripped off part of Janet Jackson's costume, exposing one of her breasts to the audience. CBS quickly cut to an aerial view of the stadium, but it was too late. Half a million viewers complained, and the federal government fined CBS $550,000. In some cultures, however, it is considered unremarkable for a woman to show her upper torso in public. Objectively speaking, such displays are neither right nor wrong.

Finally, consider an even more complex and controversial example: that of monogamous marriage. In our society, the ideal is to fall in love with, and to marry, one person, and then one is expected to remain faithful to that person forever. But aren't there other ways to pursue happiness? The advice columnist Dan Savage lists some possible drawbacks of monogamy: "boredom, despair, lack of variety, sexual death and being taken for granted." For such reasons, many people regard monogamy as an unrealistic goal—and as a goal whose pursuit would not make them happy.

What are the alternatives to this ideal? Some married couples reject monogamy by giving each other permission to have the occasional extramarital fling. Allowing one's spouse to have an affair is risky—the spouse might not come back—but greater openness in marriage might work better than our current system, in which many people feel sexually trapped and, on top of that, feel guilty for having such feelings. Other people deviate from monogamy more radically by practicing *polyamory*, which is having more than one long-term partner, with the consent of everyone involved. Polyamory includes group marriages such as "triads," involving three people, or "quads," involving four people. Some of these arrangements might work better than others, but this is not really a matter of morality. If a man's wife gives him permission to have an affair, then he isn't "cheating" on her—he isn't betraying her trust, because she has consented to the affair. Or, if four people want to live together and function as a single family, with love flowing from each to each, then there is nothing morally wrong with that. But most people in our society would disapprove of any deviation from the cultural ideal of monogamy.

The second lesson has to do with keeping an open mind. As we grow up, we develop strong feelings about things: We learn to see some types of behavior as acceptable, and other types as outrageous. Occasionally, we may find those feelings challenged. For example, we may have been taught that homosexuality is immoral, and we may feel uncomfortable around gay people. But then someone suggests that this may be prejudice; that there is nothing wrong with being gay; and that gay people are just people, like anyone else, who happen to be attracted to members of the same sex. Because we feel so strongly about this, we may find it hard to take this line of reasoning seriously.

Cultural Relativism provides an antidote for this kind of dogmatism. When he tells the story of the Greeks and Callatians, Herodotus adds:

> For if anyone, no matter who, were given the opportunity of choosing from amongst all the nations of the world the set of beliefs which he thought best, he would inevitably, after careful consideration of their relative merits, choose that of his own country. Everyone without exception believes his own native customs, and the religion he was brought up in, to be the best.

Realizing this can help broaden our minds. We can see that our feelings are not necessarily perceptions of the truth— they may be due to cultural conditioning and nothing more. Thus, when we hear it suggested that some element of our social code is *not* really the best, and we find ourselves resisting the suggestion, we might stop and remember this. Then we will be more open to discovering the truth, whatever it might be.

We can understand the appeal of Cultural Relativism, then, despite its shortcomings. It is an attractive theory because it is based on a genuine insight: that many of the practices and attitudes we find natural are really only cultural products. Moreover, keeping this thought in mind is important if we want to avoid arrogance and remain open to new ideas. These are important points, not to be taken lightly. But we can accept them without accepting the whole theory.

CHAPTER 3

*S*ubjectivism in Ethics

Take any [vicious] action. . . . Wilful murder, for instance.
Examine it in all lights, and see if you can find that matter of fact,
or real existence, which you call vice. . . . You can never find it,
till you turn your reflexion into your own breast, and find a
sentiment of [disapproval], which arises in you, toward this action.
Here is a matter of fact; but 'tis the object of feeling, not reason.

DAVID HUME, *A TREATISE OF HUMAN NATURE* (1740)

3.1. The Basic Idea of Ethical Subjectivism

In 2001 there was a mayoral election in New York, and when it
came time for the city's Gay Pride Day parade, every single Democratic and Republican candidate showed up to march. Matt
Foreman, the director of a gay rights organization, described
all the candidates at the march as "good on our issues." He
said, "In other parts of the country, the positions taken here
would be extremely unpopular, if not deadly, at the polls." The
national Republican Party apparently agrees; for decades, it has
opposed the gay rights movement.

What do people around the country actually think? Since
2001, the Gallup Poll has been asking Americans whether they
personally believe gay relations to be morally acceptable or morally wrong. In 2001, 53% of Americans considered gay relations
to be "morally wrong," with only 40% calling them "morally
acceptable." By 2011, these numbers had changed dramatically:
56% called gay relations "morally acceptable," and only 39%
deemed them "morally wrong."

People on both sides have strong feelings. Michele Bachmann, a Republican congresswoman from Minnesota, once told
a conservative audience, "If you're involved in the gay and lesbian
lifestyle, it's bondage. It is *personal* bondage, *personal* despair, and

32

personal enslavement." Bachmann and her husband offer troubled gays a way to break free from their alleged chains: they run a "Christian Counseling Center" in Minnesota, which offers its clients "Reparative Therapy" as a "cure" for homosexuality. Ms. Bachmann is an evangelical Lutheran. The Catholic view may be more nuanced, but it agrees that gay sex is wrong. According to the *Catechism of the Catholic Church*, homosexuals "do not choose their homosexual condition" and "must be accepted with respect, compassion, and sensitivity. Every sign of unjust discrimination in their regard should be avoided." Nonetheless, "homosexual acts are intrinsically disordered" and "under no circumstances can they be approved." Therefore, if gay people want to be virtuous, then they must resist their desires.

What attitude should we take? We might say that homosexuality is immoral, or we might say that it is all right. But there is a third alternative. We might say:

> People have different opinions, but where morality is concerned, there are no "facts," and no one is "right." People just feel differently, and that's all there is to it.

This is the basic thought behind Ethical Subjectivism. Ethical Subjectivism is the idea that our moral opinions are based on our feelings and nothing more. On this view, there is no such thing as "objective" right or wrong. It is a fact that some people are homosexual and some are heterosexual; but it is not a fact that one is good and the other is bad. So, when someone such as Bachmann says that homosexuality is wrong, she is not stating a fact about homosexuality. Instead, she is merely saying something about her feelings.

Of course, Ethical Subjectivism is not merely an idea about the assessment of homosexuality. It applies to all moral matters. To take a different example, it is a fact that the Nazis exterminated millions of innocent people; but according to Ethical Subjectivism, it is not a fact that what they did was evil. When we call their actions "evil," we are only saying that we have negative feelings toward them. The same applies to any moral judgment whatever.

3.2. The Evolution of the Theory

A philosophical theory may go through several stages. At first, it is put forward in simple terms, which many people find attractive. That simple formulation, however, is examined and found to have defects. At this point, some people are so impressed with the objections that they abandon the theory. Others, however, retain confidence in the basic idea, and so they refine it. For a while, it looks like they can rescue the theory. But then further arguments cast doubt on the new version. Those new objections, like the old, cause some people to abandon the idea, while others keep the faith and propose another "improved" version. The whole process of revision and criticism then begins again.

The theory of Ethical Subjectivism has developed in just this way. It began as a simple idea—in the words of David Hume, that morality is a matter of sentiment rather than fact. But as objections were raised to the theory, and its defenders tried to answer them, the theory became more sophisticated.

3.3. The First Stage: Simple Subjectivism

The simplest version of the theory is this: When a person says that something is morally good or bad, this means that he or she approves of that thing, or disapproves of it, and nothing more. In other words:

"X is morally acceptable"
"X is right"   all mean: "I (the speaker)
"X is good"   approve of X"
"X ought to be done"

And similarly:

"X is morally unacceptable"
"X is wrong"   all mean: "I (the speaker)
"X is bad"   disapprove of X"
"X ought not to be done"

We may call this version of the theory Simple Subjectivism. It expresses the basic idea of Ethical Subjectivism in a plain, uncomplicated form, and many people have found it attractive. However, it is open to some serious objections.

Simple Subjectivism Cannot Account for Disagreement. Gay rights advocate Matt Foreman does not believe that homosexuality is immoral. Congresswoman Michele Bachmann, however, believes it is. So, Foreman and Bachmann appear to disagree. But consider what Simple Subjectivism implies about this situation.

According to Simple Subjectivism, when Foreman says that homosexuality is not immoral, he is merely making a statement about his attitudes—he is saying, "I, Matt Foreman, do not disapprove of homosexuality." Would Bachmann disagree with that? No, Bachmann would agree that Foreman does not disapprove of homosexuality. At the same time, when Bachmann says that homosexuality is immoral, she is only saying, "I, Michele Bachmann, disapprove of homosexuality." And how could anyone disagree with that? Thus, according to Simple Subjectivism, there is no disagreement between them; each should acknowledge the truth of what the other is saying. Surely, though, this is incorrect, because Bachmann and Foreman *do* disagree about homosexuality.

There is a kind of eternal frustration implied by Simple Subjectivism: Bachmann and Foreman are deeply opposed to one another, yet they cannot even state their positions in a way that gets at the issue. Foreman may try to deny what Bachmann says, but according to Simple Subjectivism, he succeeds only in talking about himself.

The argument may be summarized like this: When one person says, "X is morally acceptable," and someone else says, "X is morally unacceptable," they are disagreeing. However, if Simple Subjectivism were correct, there could be no disagreement. Therefore, Simple Subjectivism cannot be correct.

Simple Subjectivism Implies That We're Always Right. We are sometimes wrong in our moral evaluations. But if Simple Subjectivism were correct, this would be impossible.

Again, consider Bachmann, who said that being gay is like being enslaved. In saying this, she probably meant that homosexuals are "slaves" to their wicked desires; they are living in the bonds of sin. According to Simple Subjectivism, when Bachmann called homosexuality "enslavement," she was merely saying that she, Bachmann, disapproves of homosexuality. Of course, she might have been speaking insincerely—it is possible that she didn't really mind homosexuality but was merely playing to her conservative audience. However, if Bachmann was speaking sincerely, then what she said was true. So long as someone is honestly representing her own feelings, her moral judgments will always be correct. But this contradicts the plain fact that we sometimes make mistakes about ethics. Therefore, Simple Subjectivism cannot be correct.

These arguments, and others like them, suggest that Simple Subjectivism is a flawed theory. In the face of such arguments, some philosophers have chosen to reject the whole idea of Ethical Subjectivism. Others, however, have worked to improve the theory.

3.4. The Second Stage: Emotivism

The improved version came to be known as Emotivism. Emotivism was popular during the mid-20th century, largely due to the work of the American philosopher Charles L. Stevenson (1908–1979).

Language, Stevenson said, is used in many ways. One way is to make statements—that is, to state facts. Thus we may say:

"Gas prices are rising."

"Lance Armstrong beat cancer and then won the Tour de France bike race seven times."

"Shakespeare wrote *Hamlet*."

In each case, we are saying something that is either true or false, and the purpose of our utterance is, typically, to convey information to the listener.

However, language is also used for other purposes. Suppose I say, "Close the door!" This utterance is neither true nor false. It is not a statement, intended to convey information; it is a command. Its purpose is to get the listener to do something.

Or consider utterances such as these, which are neither statements nor commands:

"Aaargh!"

"Way to go, Lance!"

"Damn Hamlet!"

We understand these sentences easily enough. But none of them can be true or false. (It makes no sense to say, "It is true that 'way to go, Lance'" or "It is false that 'aaargh.'") These sentences are not used to state facts or to influence behavior. Their purpose is to express the speaker's attitudes—about gas prices, about Lance Armstrong, or about Hamlet.

Now think about moral language. According to the first theory, Simple Subjectivism, moral language is about stating facts—ethical statements report the speaker's attitudes. According to Simple Subjectivism, when Bachmann says, "Homosexuality is immoral," her utterance means "I (Bachmann) disapprove of homosexuality"—a statement of fact about Bachmann's attitude.

According to Emotivism, however, moral language is not fact-stating language; it is not used to convey information or to make reports. It is used, first, as a means of influencing people's behavior. If someone says, "You shouldn't do that," he is trying to *persuade you not to do it*. Thus, his utterance is more like a command than a statement of fact; "You shouldn't do that" is like saying "Don't do that!" Also, moral language is used to express one's attitudes. Calling Lance Armstrong "a good man" is thus like saying "Way to go, Lance!" And so, when Bachmann says, "Homosexuality is immoral," emotivists interpret her utterance as equivalent to something like "Homosexuality—gross!" or "Don't be gay!"

This difference between Simple Subjectivism and Emotivism may seem trivial. But it is important. To see why, consider again the arguments against Simple Subjectivism. While those arguments were severely embarrassing to Simple Subjectivism, they are less effective against Emotivism.

1. The first argument had to do with moral disagreement. If Simple Subjectivism is correct, then when one person says, "X is morally acceptable," and someone else says, "X is morally unacceptable," they are not really disagreeing. They are, instead, talking about different things: each person is making a claim about his or her own attitude—a claim which the other person doesn't dispute. But, the argument goes, such people really do disagree. Thus, Simple Subjectivism cannot be correct.

In response, Emotivism emphasizes that disagreement comes in different forms. Compare these two kinds of disagreement:

- I believe that Lee Harvey Oswald acted alone in the assassination of President John F. Kennedy, and you believe there was a conspiracy. This is a disagreement about the facts—I believe something to be true which you believe to be false.

- I am rooting for the Atlanta Braves to win, and you want them to lose. Our beliefs are not in conflict, but our desires are—I want something to happen which you want not to happen.

In the first case, we believe different things, both of which cannot be true. Stevenson calls this *disagreement in belief.* In the second case, we want different outcomes, both of which cannot occur. Stevenson calls this *disagreement in attitude.* As Stevenson observes, we may disagree in attitude even if we don't disagree in belief. For example, you and I may have all the same beliefs regarding the Atlanta Braves baseball team: we both believe that the Braves' players are overpaid; we both believe that I am rooting for the Braves just because I am from the South; and we both believe that Atlanta is not a great baseball town. Yet despite all this common ground—despite our agreement *in belief*—we may still differ *in attitude*: I may still want the Braves to win, and you may still want them to lose.

According to Stevenson, moral disagreement is disagreement in attitude only. Matt Foreman's attitudes about homosexuality are very different from Michele Bachmann's, even if Foreman and Bachmann agree about all the facts. For Emotivism, then, moral conflict is real. By contrast, Simple Subjectivism interprets moral disagreement as disagreement in *belief*—moral judgments express beliefs about the speaker's attitudes—so, when people disagree, they must disagree about what attitudes the speaker has. However, this gets things wrong. Foreman and Bachmann do disagree about homosexuality, but they do not disagree about what their own attitudes are.

2. The second argument was that if Simple Subjectivism is correct, then we are always right in our moral judgments. But, of course, we are not always right. Therefore, Simple Subjectivism cannot be correct.

This argument is effective only because Simple Subjectivism interprets moral judgments as statements that can be true or false. "Always right" means that one's judgments are always true; and Simple Subjectivism assigns moral judgments a meaning that *will* always be true, so long as the speaker is sincere. That is why, on that theory, people turn out to be right all the time. Emotivism, on the other hand, does not interpret moral judgments as statements that are true or false. Because commands and expressions of attitude cannot be true or false, people cannot "be right" with respect to them, much less "be right all the time."

Emotivism, then, also avoids this objection to Simple Subjectivism. However, it is susceptible to a related complaint. Although we're not always right in our evaluations, we're right some of the time. Sometimes our moral judgments are true and sometimes they are false. Emotivists, however, cannot say this, because they deny that moral discourse is about stating facts.

Consider this example. On January 26, 2004, an 8-year-old girl named Katie Shelton was walking down a street in Seymour, Indiana. Suddenly she was confronted by two rottweilers, each weighing over 80 pounds. The dogs knocked Katie down and bit her repeatedly. The little girl's life, however, was saved by the heroic actions of 14-year-old Mark Friedrich, who lived nearby. When Mark saw what was going on, he rushed out of his family's house with two sticks and attacked the dogs. Predictably, Mark got bitten, but he was able to keep the dogs off Katie until a police officer arrived with a gun. Both children recovered from their wounds (the dogs were not so lucky).

Now suppose that, upon hearing this story, someone said that Mark Friedrich acted badly: "If he was a good kid, he would have minded his own business and stayed in his house." As long as this strange person was speaking sincerely, the Simple Subjectivist would have to say that his moral judgment was *true*. The emotivist's position is different, but like the Simple Subjectivist, she is barred from saying that this person's judgment is false. She must say that he is merely expressing his feelings.

Although Emotivism is an improvement on Simple Subjectivism, both theories imply that our moral judgments are, in a sense, beyond reproach. For Simple Subjectivism, our judgments cannot be criticized because they will always be true. For Emotivism, our moral judgments cannot be criticized because they are not judgments at all; they are mere expressions of attitude, which cannot be false. That is one problem for Emotivism. Another problem is that Emotivism cannot explain the role reason plays in ethics.

3.5. The Role of Reason in Ethics

If someone says, "I like peaches," she does not need to have a reason; she may be making a statement about her personal taste and nothing more. But moral judgments are different. If someone tells you that a particular act would be wrong, you may ask why, and if there is no satisfactory answer, then you may reject that advice as unfounded. A moral judgment—or for that matter, any kind of value judgment—must be supported by good reasons. Any adequate theory of ethics should be able to explain how reasons can support moral judgments.

What do emotivists say about reasons? Remember that for the emotivist, moral judgments have two functions: to express one's attitudes, and to try to influence other people's attitudes and conduct. Can the expressive function of moral language find a place for reasons? Insofar as moral judgments are mere expressions of attitude, they are like personal preferences. When I say, "Letting people be free is morally better than enslaving them," the emotivist hears this as similar to "Peaches are better than apples." The emotivist can recognize some differences between those two utterances. However, they are basically alike. Reason can play no important role here.

Thus, emotivists have usually looked to the command function of moral language to find a role for reasons. Suppose I had said to you in 2008, "You shouldn't vote for Barack Obama." If this utterance is like a command—if it is like saying, "Don't vote for Obama"—then what role can reasons play in such a judgment? If I am trying to influence your conduct, then perhaps the emotivist should say that a reason is any consideration that will influence your conduct. But consider what this means. Suppose I know that you are prejudiced against Muslims. And I say, "Obama, you know, is a Muslim." That does the trick; you now decide not to vote for Obama. For the emotivist, the claim that Obama is a Muslim would be, given the right audience, a moral reason not to vote for him. In fact, Stevenson takes exactly this view. In his classic work *Ethics and Language* (1944), he says, "*Any* statement about *any* matter of fact which *any* speaker considers likely to alter attitudes may be adduced as a reason for or against an ethical judgment."

Obviously, something has gone wrong. Not just any claim can count as a reason in support of just any judgment. For one thing, it must be relevant to the judgment, and psychological influence does not always bring relevance with it. Being Muslim is irrelevant to one's ability to be a good president, regardless of the psychological connections in anyone's mind. Also, to be a legitimate reason, a claim must be true, and yet false claims can be persuasive. President Obama is not in fact a Muslim.

There are two lessons to be learned from this. The small lesson is that a particular moral theory, Emotivism, is flawed, which casts doubt on the whole idea of Ethical Subjectivism. The larger lesson has to do with the importance of reason in ethics.

Hume said that if we examine wicked actions—"wilful murder, for instance"—we will find no "matter of fact" corresponding to the wickedness. The universe, apart from our attitudes, contains no such facts. What can we conclude from this? Admittedly, value is not a tangible thing like a planet or a spoon. But this does not mean that ethics has no objective basis. A fundamental mistake, which many people fall into, is to assume just two possibilities:

1. There are moral facts, in the same way that there are planets and spoons.
2. Our values are nothing more than the expression of our subjective feelings.

This is a mistake because it overlooks a third possibility. People have not only feelings but reason, and that makes a big difference. It may be that

3. Moral truths are truths of reason; that is, a moral judgment is true if it is backed by better reasons than the alternatives.

On this view, moral truths are objective in the sense that they are true independently of what we might want or think. We cannot make something good or bad just by wishing it so, because our will cannot determine what the reasons are. And this also explains our fallibility: We can be wrong about what is good or bad because we can be wrong about what reason recommends. Reason says what it says, regardless of our opinions or desires.

3.6. Are There Proofs in Ethics?

If Ethical Subjectivism is not true, why are so many people attracted to it? One reason is that science provides our paradigm of objectivity, and when we compare ethics to science, ethics seems lacking. For example, there are proofs in science, but there are no proofs in ethics. We can prove that the earth is round, that dinosaurs lived before humans, and that there is no largest prime number. But we can't prove that abortion is acceptable or unacceptable.

The general idea that moral judgments can't be proved sounds appealing. Anyone who has ever argued about something like abortion knows how frustrating it can be to try to "prove" one's opinion. However, if we inspect this idea more closely, it turns out to be flawed.

Suppose we consider something much simpler than abortion. A student says that a test was unfair. This is clearly a moral judgment—fairness is a basic moral value. Can this judgment be proved? The student might point out that the test covered a lot of material that was trivial while ignoring material the teacher had stressed as important. The test also included questions that were not covered in either the readings or the class discussions. Moreover, the test was so long that nobody could finish it in the time allowed.

Suppose all this is true. And further suppose that the teacher, when asked to explain, can offer no defense. In fact, the teacher, who is rather inexperienced, seems confused about the whole thing. Now, hasn't the student proved that the test was unfair? What more in the way of proof could we want? It is easy to think of other examples that make the same point:

- *Jones is a bad man:* Jones is a habitual liar; he toys with people; he cheats at cards; he once killed someone in a dispute over 27 cents; and so on.
- *Dr. Smith is irresponsible:* He bases his diagnoses on superficial considerations; he refuses to listen to other doctors' advice; he drinks beer before performing delicate surgery; and so on.
- *A certain used-car dealer is unethical:* She conceals defects in her cars; she tries to pressure people into paying too much; she runs misleading ads on the Web; and so on.

The process of giving reasons might even be taken one step further. If we criticize Jones for being a habitual liar, we can go on to explain why lying is bad. Lying is bad, first, because it harms people. If I give you false information, and you rely on it, things may go wrong for you in all sorts of ways. Second, lying is bad because it is a violation of trust. Trusting another person means leaving oneself vulnerable and unprotected. When I trust you, I simply believe what you say, without taking precautions; and when you lie, you take advantage of my trust. And finally, the rule requiring truthfulness is necessary for society to exist—if we could not assume that other people would speak truthfully, communication would be impossible, and if communication were impossible, society would fall apart.

So we can support our judgments with good reasons, and we can explain why those reasons matter. If we can do all this, and, for an encore, show that no comparable case can be made on the other side, what more in the way of "proof" could anyone want? In the face of all this, it is absurd to say that ethical judgments are nothing but "opinions."

Nevertheless, the impression that moral judgments are "unprovable" is remarkably persistent. Why do people believe this? Three points might be raised.

First, when proof is demanded, people often want scientific proof. They want something like experimental verification, and because ethical judgments cannot be experimentally tested, they say there is no proof. But in ethics, rational thinking consists in giving reasons, analyzing arguments, setting out and justifying principles, and so on. The fact that ethical reasoning differs from scientific reasoning does not make it deficient.

Second, when we think about proving our ethical opinions, we tend to think of the most difficult issues. The question of abortion, for example, is enormously complicated. If we consider only issues like abortion, it is easy to believe that "proof" in ethics is impossible. But the same could be said of the sciences. There are complicated matters that physicists cannot agree on; and if we focused entirely on them, we might conclude that there are no proofs in physics. But, of course, there are many simpler issues on which all physicists agree. Similarly, in ethics, there are many simple issues about which all reasonable people agree.

Finally, it is easy to run together two matters that are really very different:

1. Proving an opinion to be correct
2. Persuading someone to accept your proof

When your argument fails to persuade your audience, it is tempting to think, "Well, that argument didn't work." But the argument might have failed merely because your audience was stubborn, or biased, or not really listening. As a proof, your argument might have been perfect.

3.7. The Question of Homosexuality

Let's return to the dispute about homosexuality. If we consider the relevant reasons, what do we find? The most pertinent fact is that gays are pursuing the only kind of life that can make them happy. Sex, after all, is a particularly strong urge, and few people can be happy without satisfying their sexual needs. But we should not focus solely on sex. Homosexuality is not merely about who you have sex with; it's about who you fall in love with. Gay people fall in love in the same way that straight people do. And, like straights, gays often want to be with, live with, and build a life with, the person they love. To say that homosexuals shouldn't act on their desires is thus to condemn them to frustrating lives. It should be added that gay people cannot avoid the frustration by choosing to become straight. Both homosexuals and heterosexuals discover who they are, once they reach a certain age; nobody decides which sex to be attracted to.

Why do people oppose gay rights? Some people think that homosexuals pose a danger to others. Often the charge, whether stated or not, is that gay men are likely to be child molesters. There have, for example, been several campaigns in America to get gay public schoolteachers fired, and the fear of pedophilia has always loomed large in these discussions. Congresswoman Bachmann exploited this fear when she said of gay marriage, "This is a very serious matter, because it is our children who are the prize for this community—[the gay community] are specifically targeting our children." Such a fear, however, has never had any basis in fact. It is a mere stereotype, like the idea that blacks are lazy or that Muslims are terrorists. There is no difference between gays and heterosexuals in their moral characters or in their contributions to society.

The most common objection to homosexuality may be that it is "unnatural." What should we make of this? To assess the argument, we need to know what "unnatural" means. There seem to be three possibilities.

First, "unnatural" might be taken as a statistical notion. In this sense, a human quality is unnatural if most people don't have it. Being gay would be unnatural in this sense, but so would being left-handed, being tall, and even being immensely nice. Clearly, this is no reason to criticize homosexuality. Rare qualities are often good.

Second, the meaning of "unnatural" might be connected with the idea of a thing's *purpose*. The parts of our bodies seem to serve particular purposes. The purpose of the eyes is to see, and the purpose of the heart is to pump blood. Similarly, the purpose of our genitals is to procreate: Sex is for making babies. It may be argued, then, that gay sex is unnatural because it is sexual activity that is divorced from its natural purpose.

This seems to express what many people have in mind when they object to homosexuality as unnatural. However, if gay sex were condemned for this reason, then a number of other, widely accepted practices would also have to be condemned: masturbation, oral sex, sex using condoms, and even sex by women during pregnancy or after menopause. These practices would be just as "unnatural" (and, presumably, just as bad) as gay sex. But there is no reason to accept these conclusions, because this whole line of reasoning is faulty. It rests on the assumption that *it is wrong to use parts of one's body for anything other than their natural purposes.* Why should we accept that assumption? The "purpose" of the eyes is to see; is it therefore wrong to use one's eyes for flirting or for giving a signal? The "purpose" of the fingers may be to grasp and poke; is it therefore wrong to snap one's fingers to get someone's attention? The idea that things should be used only in "natural" ways cannot be maintained, and so this version of the argument fails.

Third, because the word *unnatural* has a sinister sound, it might be understood simply as a term of evaluation. Perhaps it means something like "contrary to what a person ought to be." But if that is what "unnatural" means, then to say that homosexuality is wrong because it is unnatural would be vacuous. It would be like saying that homosexuality is wrong because it is wrong. That sort of empty remark provides no reason for condemning anything.

The idea that homosexuality is unnatural, and so it must be immoral, seems right to many people. Nevertheless, it is an unsound argument. It fails on every interpretation.

But what about the claim, often made, that homosexuality is "contrary to family values"? James Dobson, founder of the conservative Christian group, Focus on the Family, told his followers: "For more than 40 years, the homosexual activist movement has sought to implement a master plan that has had as its centerpiece the utter destruction of the family." But how, exactly, are homosexuals trying to destroy the family? Gay activists are actually trying to *expand* the family. They do not wish to take any rights away from heterosexual couples. Instead, they want to make it easier for gays to form families— they support same-sex marriage, domestic partner benefits, the right of gay couples to adopt children, and so on. Gays find it ironic that supporters of "the family" want to prevent them from having families.

Perhaps all this talk of "family values" really amounts to saying, "Let's make sure we don't have families *like that.*" But if so, then the question arises: What is wrong with a family in which the children are raised by two mothers, or two fathers? Common sense suggests that two parents are better than one: raising a child is a huge task, and two people can perform big tasks more easily than one. But even if the *number* of parents in a household matters, it is not clear why their gender should. The largest study of gay families is the U.S. National Longitudinal Lesbian Family Study, which has followed a group of gay mothers since the 1980s. Their data suggest that the teenage children of lesbians actually do *better* than teenagers from traditional homes. Sometimes the children of gay parents are made fun of at school, and this is difficult for them. But, in general, these children have fewer behavioral problems, and they do better both socially and academically than their peers. There is no good reason to be against gay families.

Meanwhile, homosexuals in America continue to be disadvantaged. Sometimes the disadvantage is a matter of law. Legally, heterosexuals can tie the knot in any state, but gay marriage exists in only a half-dozen states. Moreover, the federal government does not recognize gay marriage as legitimate, and so it provides marital benefits to heterosexual couples only. There are hundreds of such benefits, including the social security benefits that a spouse may receive after the other spouse's death. Finally, in Florida and Arkansas, gay people cannot legally adopt children, although, of course, heterosexuals can. The law in America certainly discriminates against gays. Yet, in many other places, the laws are even more extreme.

In 76 countries, gay sex is illegal. In some countries, the punishment is death.

Apart from the law, there are social drawbacks to being gay in America. It is tough to grow up in a place where four-tenths of your neighbors believe that something is wrong with you. Even worse, you find that some of your neighbors are hateful—they are repulsed by you and see you as less than human. It is especially sad when a young person who has been taught to despise homosexuality begins to realize that he or she is gay. Many gays, whether out of fear or shame, choose to live in the closet. But in the long run, it is almost impossible to hide one's sexuality from friends, family members, and co-workers. Gays in America lead stressful lives. Among American college students, gays are twice as likely to attempt suicide as their straight classmates. And *closeted* gays are *six times* more likely to try it.

One more argument must be discussed, namely, that homosexuality is condemned in the Bible. For example, Leviticus 18:22 says, "You may not lie with a man as with a woman; it is an abomination." Some commentators have said that, contrary to appearances, the Bible is really not so harsh toward homosexuality; and they explain how each relevant passage (there seem to be nine of them) should be understood. But suppose we accept that the Bible condemns homosexuality. What may we infer from this? Are we supposed to believe what the Bible says, simply because it says it?

This question will offend some people. To question the Bible, they believe, is to challenge the word of God. And this, they think, is an act of arrogance coming from creatures who should be showing gratitude to the Almighty. Questioning the Bible can also make people feel uncomfortable, because it may seem to challenge their whole way of life. However, thoughts like these cannot hold us back. Philosophy *is* about questioning whole ways of life. When the argument is given that homosexuality must be wrong because the Bible says so, this argument must be assessed on its own terms.

The problem with the argument is that, if we look at *other* things the Bible says, it does not appear to be a reliable guide to morality. Leviticus condemns homosexuality, but it also forbids eating sheep's fat (7:23), letting a woman into the church's sanctuary who has recently given birth (12:2–5), and seeing your uncle naked. The latter, like homosexuality, is deemed an abomination (18:14, 26). Even worse, Leviticus condemns to death those who curse their parents (20:9) and those who commit adultery (20:10). It says that a priest's daughter, if she "plays the whore," shall be burned alive (21:9), and it says that we may purchase slaves from nearby nations (25:44). In Exodus, it even says that it's okay to beat your slaves, so long as you don't kill them (21:20–21).

The point of all this is not to ridicule the Bible; the Bible, in fact, contains much that is true and wise. But we can conclude from examples like these that the Bible is not always right. And because it's not always right, we can't conclude that homosexuality is an abomination just because it says so in Leviticus.

At any rate, nothing can be morally right or wrong *simply* because an authority says so. If the precepts in a sacred text are not arbitrary, there must be some reason for them—we should be able to ask *why* the Bible condemns homosexuality and then to get an answer. That answer will then give the real explanation of why the thing is wrong.

But the main point of this chapter is not about homosexuality. The main point concerns the nature of moral thinking. Moral thinking and moral conduct are a matter of weighing reasons and being guided by them. But being guided by reason is very different from following one's feelings. When we have strong feelings, we may be tempted to ignore reason and go with the feelings. But in doing so, we would be opting out of moral thinking altogether. That is why, in focusing on attitudes and feelings, Ethical Subjectivism seems to be going in the wrong direction.

CHAPTER 4

Does Morality Depend on Religion?

The Good consists in always doing what God wills at any particular moment.

EMIL BRUNNER, *THE DIVINE IMPERATIVE* (1947)

I respect deities. I do not rely upon them.

MUSASHI MIYAMOTO, AT ICHIJOJI TEMPLE (ca. 1608)

4.1. The Presumed Connection between Morality and Religion

In 1995 the American Civil Liberties Union (ACLU) sued Judge Roy Moore of Gadsden, Alabama, for displaying the Ten Commandments in his courtroom. Such a display, the ACLU said, violates the separation of church and state, which is guaranteed by the U.S. Constitution. The ACLU might not have liked Moore, but Alabama voters did. In 2000, Moore successfully campaigned to become chief justice of the Alabama Supreme Court, running on a promise to "restore the moral foundation of law." Thus the "Ten Commandments judge" became the most powerful jurist in the state of Alabama.

Moore was not through making his point, however. In the wee hours of July 31, 2001, he had a granite monument to the Ten Commandments installed in the Alabama state judicial building. This monument weighed over 5,000 pounds, and anyone entering the building could not miss it. Moore was sued again, but the people were behind him: 77% of Americans thought that he should be allowed to display his monument. Yet the law did not agree. When Moore disobeyed a court order to remove the monument, the Alabama Court of the Judiciary fired him, saying that he had placed himself above the law. Moore, however, believed that he was putting *God* above the law.

The United States is a religious country. Nearly 80% of Americans say they believe in God, and another 12% say they believe in a universal spirit or higher power. The main religion in America is Christianity; 41% of Americans report believing that Jesus Christ will return to earth by 2050. In America, members of the Christian clergy are often treated as moral experts: Hospitals ask them to sit on ethics committees; reporters interview them on the moral dimensions of a story; and churchgoers look to them for guidance. The clergy even help decide whether movies will be rated "G," "PG," "PG-13," "R," or "NC-17." Priests and ministers are assumed to be wise counselors who will give sound moral advice.

Why are the clergy regarded in this way? The reason is not that they have proven themselves to be better or wiser than other people—as a group, they seem to be neither better nor worse than the rest of us. There is a deeper reason why they are thought to have special moral insight. In popular thinking, morality and religion are inseparable: People commonly believe that morality can be understood only in the context of religion. Thus the clergy are assumed to be authorities on morality.

It is not hard to see why people think this. When viewed from a nonreligious perspective, the universe seems to be a cold, meaningless place, devoid of value and purpose. In his essay "A Free Man's Worship," written in 1902, Bertrand Russell expressed what he called the "scientific" view of the world:

> That Man is the product of causes which had no prevision of the end they were achieving; that his origin, his growth, his hopes and fears, his loves and his beliefs, are but the outcome of accidental collocations of atoms; that no fire, no heroism, no intensity of thought and feeling, can preserve an individual life beyond the grave; that all the labours of the ages, all the devotion, all the inspiration, all the noonday brightness of human genius, are destined to extinction in the vast death of the solar system, and that the whole temple of Man's achievement must inevitably be buried beneath the debris of a universe in ruins—all these things, if not quite beyond dispute, are yet so nearly certain that no philosophy which rejects them can hope to stand.

From a religious perspective, however, things look very different. Judaism and Christianity teach that the world was created by a loving, all-powerful God to provide a home for us. We, in turn, were created in his image, to be his children. Thus, the world is not devoid of meaning and purpose. It is, instead, the arena in which God's plans are realized. What could be more natural, then, than to think of "morality" as part of religion, while the atheist's world has no place for values?

4.2. The Divine Command Theory

Christians, Jews, and Muslims all believe that God has told us to obey certain rules of conduct. God does not force these rules on us. He created us as free agents; so, we may choose what to do. But if we live as we should, then we must follow God's laws. This idea has been expanded into a theory known as the Divine Command Theory. The basic idea is that God decides what is right and wrong. Actions that God commands are morally required; actions that God forbids are morally wrong; and all other actions are permissible or merely morally neutral.

This theory has a number of attractive features. It immediately solves the old problem of the objectivity of ethics. Ethics is not merely a matter of personal feeling or social custom. Whether something is right or wrong is perfectly objective: It is right if God commands it and wrong if God forbids it. Moreover, the Divine Command Theory explains why anyone should bother with morality. Why not forget about "ethics" and just look out for yourself? If immorality is the violation of God's commandments, there is an easy answer: On the day of final reckoning, you will be held accountable.

There are, however, serious problems with the theory. Of course, atheists would not accept it, because they do not believe that God exists. But there are difficulties even for believers. The main problem was identified by Plato, a Greek philosopher who lived 400 years before Jesus of Nazareth. Plato's books are written as conversations, or dialogues, in which Plato's teacher Socrates is always the main speaker. In one of them, the *Euthyphro*, there is a discussion of whether "right" can be defined as "what the gods command." Socrates is skeptical and asks, Is conduct right because the gods command it, or do the gods command it because it is right? This is one of the most famous questions in the history of philosophy. The British philosopher Antony Flew (1923–2010) suggests that "one good test of a person's aptitude for philosophy is to discover whether he can grasp [the] force and point" of this question.

Socrates's question is about whether God *makes* the moral truths true or whether he merely *recognizes* that they're true. There's a big difference between these options. I know that the Burj Khalifa building in the United Arab Emirates is the tallest building in the world; I recognize that fact. However, I did not make it true. Rather, it was made true by the designers and builders in the city of Dubai. Is God's relation to ethics like my relation to the Burj Khalifa building or like the relation of the builders? This question poses a dilemma, and either way out leads to trouble.

First, we might say that *right conduct is right because God commands it.* For example, according to Exodus 20:16, God commands us to be truthful. Thus, we should be truthful simply because God requires it. God's command makes truthfulness right, just as the builders of a skyscraper make the building tall. This is the Divine Command Theory. It is almost the theory of Shakespeare's character Hamlet. Hamlet said that nothing is good or bad, but thinking makes it so. According to the Divine Command Theory, nothing is good or bad, except when *God's* thinking makes it so.

This idea encounters several difficulties.

1. *This conception of morality is mysterious.* What does it mean to say that God "makes" truthfulness right? It is easy enough to understand how physical objects are made, at least in principle. We have all made something, if only a sand castle or a peanut-butter-and-jelly sandwich. But making truthfulness right is not like that; it could not be done by rearranging things in the physical environment. How, then, could it be done? No one knows.

To see the problem, consider some wretched case of child abuse. On the theory we're now considering, God could make *that* instance of child abuse right—not by turning a slap into a friendly pinch of the cheek, but *by commanding that the slap is right.* This proposal defies human understanding. How could merely saying, or commanding, that the slap is right make it right? If true, this conception of morality would be a mystery.

2. *This conception of morality makes God's commands arbitrary.* We assume that God has good reasons for what he does.

But suppose God commands truthfulness to be right. On this theory, he could have given different commands just as easily. He could have commanded us to be liars, and then lying, and not truthfulness, would be right. After all, before God issues his commands, no reasons for or against lying exist—*God is the one who creates the reasons.* And so, from a moral point of view, God's commands are arbitrary. He could command anything whatsoever. This result may seem not only unacceptable but impious from a religious point of view.

3. *This conception of morality provides the wrong reasons for moral principles.* There are many things wrong with child abuse: It is malicious; it involves the unnecessary infliction of pain; it can have unwanted long-term psychological effects; and so on. However, the theory we're now considering cannot recognize any of these reasons as important. All it cares about, in the end, is whether child abuse runs counter to God's commands.

There are two ways of confirming that something is wrong here. First, notice something the theory implies: *If God didn't exist, child abuse wouldn't be wrong.* After all, if God didn't exist, then God wouldn't be around to make child abuse wrong. However, child abuse would still be malicious, so it would still be wrong. Thus, the Divine Command Theory fails. Second, keep in mind that even a religious person might be genuinely in doubt as to what God has commanded. After all, religious texts disagree with each other, and sometimes there seem to be inconsistencies even within a single text. So, a person might be in doubt as to what God's will really is. However, a person needn't be in doubt as to whether child abuse is wrong. What God has commanded is one thing; whether hitting children is wrong is another.

There is a way to avoid these troublesome consequences. We can take the second of Socrates's options. We need not say that right conduct is right because God commands it. Instead, we may say that God commands us to do certain things *because they are right.* God, who is infinitely wise, recognizes that truthfulness is better than deceitfulness, and so he commands us to be truthful; he sees that killing is wrong, and so he commands us not to kill; and so on for the other moral rules.

If we take this option, we avoid the consequences that spoiled the first alternative. We needn't worry about how God makes it wrong to lie, because he doesn't. God's commands are not arbitrary; they are the result of his wisdom in knowing what is best. Furthermore, we are not saddled with the wrong explanations for our moral principles; rather, we are free to appeal to whatever justifications of them seem appropriate.

Unfortunately, this second option has a different drawback. In taking it, we abandon the theological conception of right and wrong. When we say that God commands us to be truthful *because* truthfulness is right, we acknowledge a standard that is independent of God's will. The rightness exists prior to God's command and is the reason for the command. Thus, if we want to know why we should be truthful, the reply "because God commands it" does not really tell us. We may still ask, "*Why* does God command it?" and the answer to *that* question will provide the ultimate reason.

Many religious people believe that they must accept a theological conception of right and wrong because it would be sacrilegious not to do so. They feel, somehow, that if they believe in God, then right and wrong must be understood in terms of God's wishes. Our arguments, however, suggest that the Divine Command Theory is not only untenable but impious. And, in fact, some of the greatest theologians have rejected the theory for just this reason. Thinkers such as Saint Thomas Aquinas connect morality with religion in a different way.

4.3. The Theory of Natural Law

In the history of Christian thought, the dominant theory of ethics is not the Divine Command Theory. That honor instead goes to the Theory of Natural Law. This theory has three main parts.

1. The Theory of Natural Law rests on a particular view of the world. On this view, the world has a rational order, with values and purposes built into its very nature. This conception derives from the Greeks, whose way of understanding the world dominated Western thinking for over 1,700 years. The Greeks believed that *everything in nature has a purpose.*

Aristotle (384–322 B.C.) built this idea into his system of thought when he said that, in order to understand anything, four questions must be asked: What is it? What is it made of? How did it come to be? And what is it for? The answers might be: This is a knife; it is made of metal; it was made by a craftsman; and it is used for cutting. Aristotle assumed that the last question—What is it for?—could be asked of anything whatever. "Nature," he said, "belongs to the class of causes which act for the sake of something."

Obviously, artifacts such as knives have purposes, because craftsmen have built them with a purpose in mind. But what about natural objects that we do not make? Aristotle believed that they have purposes, too. One of his examples was that we have teeth so that we can chew. Biological examples are quite persuasive; each part of our bodies does seem, intuitively, to have a special purpose—our eyes are for seeing, our heart is for pumping blood, our skin is there to protect us, and so on. But Aristotle's claim was not limited to organic beings. According to him, *everything* has a purpose. To take a different sort of example, he thought that rain falls so that plants can grow. He considered other alternatives, such as that the rain falls "of necessity" and that this helps the plants only "by coincidence." However, he rejected them.

The world, therefore, is an orderly, rational system, with each thing having its own proper place and serving its own special purpose. There is a neat hierarchy: The rain exists for the sake of the plants, the plants exist for the sake of the animals, and the animals exist—of course—for the sake of people. Aristotle says: "If then we are right in believing that nature makes nothing without some end in view, nothing to no purpose, it must be that nature has made all things specifically for the sake of man." This worldview is stunningly anthropocentric, or human-centered. But Aristotle was hardly alone in having such thoughts; almost every important thinker in our history has advanced such a thesis. Humans are a remarkably vain species.

The Christian thinkers who came later found this worldview congenial. Only one thing was missing: God. Thus, the Christian thinkers said that the rain falls to help the plants *because that is what God intended,* and the animals are for human use because *that is what God made them for.* Values and purposes were thus conceived to be part of the divine plan.

2. A corollary to this way of thinking is that the "laws of nature" describe not only how things *are* but also how things *ought to be.* The world is in harmony when things serve their natural purposes. When they do not, or cannot, things have gone wrong. Eyes that cannot see are defective, and drought is a natural evil; the badness of both is explained by reference to natural law. But there are also implications for human conduct. Moral rules are now viewed as deriving from the laws of nature. Some ways of behaving are said to be "natural" while others are said to be "unnatural"; and "unnatural" acts are regarded as morally wrong.

Consider, for example, the duty of beneficence. We are morally required to care about our neighbors. Why? According to the Theory of Natural Law, beneficence is natural for us, given the kind of creatures we are. We are by nature social and need the company of other people. Someone who does not care at all for others—who really does not care, through and through—is seen as deranged. Modern psychiatry says that such people suffer from *antisocial personality disorder*, and such people are commonly called *psychopaths* or *sociopaths*. A malicious personality is defective, just as eyes are defective if they cannot see. And, it may be added, this is true because we were created by God, with a specific "human" nature, as part of his overall plan.

The endorsement of beneficence is relatively uncontroversial. Natural-law theory has also been used, however, to support more contentious moral views. Religious thinkers often condemn "deviant" sexual practices, and they usually justify this by appealing to the Theory of Natural Law. If everything has a purpose, what is the purpose of sex? The obvious answer is procreation. Sexual activity that is not connected with making babies can therefore be seen as "unnatural," and practices like masturbation and gay sex may be condemned for this reason. This view of sex dates back at least to Saint Augustine (A.D. 354–430), and it is explicit in the writings of Saint Thomas Aquinas (1225–1274). The moral theology of the Catholic Church is based on natural-law theory.

Outside the Catholic Church, the Theory of Natural Law has few advocates today. It is generally rejected for three reasons.

First, the idea that "what's natural is good" seems open to obvious counterexamples. Sometimes what's natural is bad. People naturally care much more about themselves than about strangers, but this is regrettable. Disease occurs naturally, but disease is bad. Children are naturally self-centered, but parents don't think this is a good thing.

Second, the Theory of Natural Law seems to confuse "is" and "ought." In the 18th century, David Hume pointed out that *what is the case* and *what ought to be the case* are logically different notions, and no conclusion about one follows from the other. We can say that people are naturally disposed to be beneficent, but it does not follow that they *ought* to be beneficent. Similarly, it may be true that sex produces babies, but it does not follow that sex *ought* or *ought not* to be engaged in only for that purpose. Facts are one thing; values are another.

Third, the Theory of Natural Law is now widely rejected because its view of the world conflicts with modern science. The world as described by Galileo, Newton, and Darwin has no need for "facts" about right and wrong. Their explanations of natural phenomena make no reference to values or purposes. What happens just happens, due to the laws of cause and effect. If the rain benefits the plants, this is because the plants have evolved by the laws of natural selection in a rainy climate.

Thus, modern science gives us a picture of the world as a realm of facts, where the only "natural laws" are the laws of physics, chemistry, and biology, working blindly and without purpose. Whatever values may be, they are not part of the natural order. As for the idea that "nature has made all things specifically for the sake of man," well, that is only vanity. To the extent that one accepts the worldview of modern science, one will be skeptical of the Theory of Natural Law. It is no accident that the theory was a product, not of modern thought, but of the Middle Ages.

3. The third part of the theory addresses the question of moral knowledge. How can we determine what is right and what is wrong? The Divine Command Theory says that we must consult God's commandments. The Theory of Natural Law gives a different answer. The "natural laws" that specify what we should do are laws of reason, which we are able to grasp because God has given us the power to understand them. Therefore, the Theory of Natural Law endorses the familiar idea that the right thing to do is whatever action has the best reasons backing it up. To use the traditional terminology, moral judgments are "dictates of reason." As Saint Thomas Aquinas, the greatest natural-law theorist, wrote in his masterpiece the *Summa Theologica,* "To disparage the dictate of reason is equivalent to condemning the command of God."

This means that the religious believer has no special access to moral truth. The believer and the nonbeliever are in the same position. God has given everyone the ability to listen to reason and follow its directives. In an important sense, this leaves morality independent of religion. Religious belief does not affect the calculation of what is best, and the results of moral inquiry are religiously "neutral." Even though they may disagree about religion, believers and nonbelievers inhabit the same moral universe.

4.4. Religion and Particular Moral Issues

Some religious people will find the preceding discussion unsatisfying. It will seem too abstract to have any bearing on their actual lives. For them, the connection between morality and religion is an immediate, practical matter that centers on particular moral issues. It doesn't matter whether right and wrong are understood in terms of God's will or whether moral laws are laws of nature. What matters are the moral teachings of one's religion. The Scriptures and the church leaders are regarded as authorities; if one is truly faithful, one must accept what they say. Many Christians, for example, believe that they must oppose abortion because the church condemns it and (they assume) the Scriptures do too.

Are there distinctively religious positions on major moral issues that believers must accept? The rhetoric of the pulpit suggests so. But there is good reason to think otherwise.

For one thing, it is often difficult to find specific moral guidance in the Scriptures. We face different problems than our ancestors faced 2,000 years ago; thus, the Scriptures may be silent on matters that seem pressing to us. The Bible does contain a number of general precepts—for example, to love one's neighbor and to treat others as one wishes to be treated. And those are fine principles, which have practical application in our lives. However, it is not clear what they imply about the rights of workers, or the extinction of species, or the funding of medical research, and so on.

Another problem is that the Scriptures and church tradition are often ambiguous. Authorities disagree, leaving the believer in the awkward position of having to choose which element of the tradition to accept. For instance, the New Testament condemns being rich, and there is a long tradition of self-denial and charitable giving that affirms this teaching. But there is also an obscure Old Testament figure named Jabez who asked God to "enlarge my territories" (1 Chronicles 4:10), and God did. A recent book urging Christians to adopt Jabez as their model became a best-seller.

Thus, when people say that their moral views come from their religion, they are often mistaken. What's really going on is this. They are making up their minds about the moral issues and then interpreting the Scriptures, or church tradition, in a way that supports the conclusions they've already reached. Of course, this does not happen in every case, but it seems fair to say that it happens a lot. The question of riches is one example; abortion is another.

In the debate over abortion, religious issues are never far from the discussion. Religious conservatives hold that the fetus is a person from the moment of conception, and so abortion is murder. The fetus, they believe, is not merely a *potential* person but is an *actual* person, possessing a full-fledged right to life. Liberals, of course, deny this—they say that the fetus is something less than that, at least at the beginning of the pregnancy.

The abortion debate is complex, but we are concerned only with how it relates to religion. Conservatives sometimes say that fetal life is sacred. Is that the Christian view? *Must* Christians condemn abortion? To answer those questions, one might look to the Scriptures or to church tradition.

The Scriptures. It is difficult to derive a prohibition against abortion from either the Jewish or the Christian Scriptures. Certain passages, however, are often quoted by conservatives because they seem to suggest that fetuses have full human status. One of the most frequently cited passages is from the first chapter of Jeremiah, in which Jeremiah quotes God as saying, "Before I formed you in the womb I knew you, and before you were born I consecrated you." These words are presented as though they were God's endorsement of the conservative position: it is wrong to kill the unborn because the unborn are consecrated to God.

In context, however, these words obviously mean something different. Suppose we read the whole passage in which they occur:

> Now the word of the Lord came to me, saying, "Before I formed you in the womb I knew you, and before you were born I consecrated you; I appointed you a prophet to the nations."

> Then I said, "Ah, Lord God! Behold, I do not know
> how to speak, for I am only a youth." But the Lord said
> to me,
> "Do not say, 'I am only a youth'; for to all to whom I
> send you, you shall go, and whatever I command you, you
> shall speak. Be not afraid of them, for I am with you to
> deliver you."

The sanctity of fetal life is not discussed in this passage. Instead, Jeremiah is asserting his authority as a prophet. He is saying, in effect, "God authorized me to speak for him; even though I resisted, he insisted." But Jeremiah puts the point more poetically; he says that God had intended him to be a prophet even before he was born.

This often happens when the Scriptures are cited in connection with controversial moral issues. A few words are lifted from a passage that is concerned with something else entirely, and those words are then construed in a way that supports a favored moral position. When this happens, is it accurate to say that the person is "following the moral teachings of the Bible"? Or is it more accurate to say that he has searched the Scriptures to find support for a moral view he already believes, and then has read the desired conclusion into the Scriptures? If the latter, it suggests an arrogant attitude—the attitude that God himself must share one's own moral opinions!

Other biblical passages seem to support a *liberal* view of abortion. Three times the death penalty is recommended for women who have had sex out of wedlock, even though killing the woman would also kill her fetus (Genesis 38:24; Leviticus 21:9; Deuteronomy 22:20–21). This suggests that the fetus has no right to life. Also, in Exodus 21, God tells Moses that the penalty for murder is death; however, the penalty for causing a woman to miscarry is only a fine. The Law of Israel seemed to regard the fetus as something less than a person.

Church Tradition.   Today, the Catholic Church strongly opposes abortion. When the Pope visits America, where abortions are performed routinely, his main message is always: *Stop killing unborn children.* In many Protestant churches, too, abortion is routinely denounced from the pulpit. It is no surprise, then, that many people feel that they must condemn abortion "for religious reasons," regardless of how Scripture is interpreted. What lies behind the Church's current position on abortion?

To some extent, the Vatican has always opposed abortion for the same reason that it has always condemned condoms, birth control pills, and other forms of contraception: All of these activities thwart natural processes. According to natural-law theory, sex is supposed to lead to the birth of a healthy baby. Condoms and birth control pills prevent this from happening by preventing pregnancy; and abortion, whenever it occurs, puts a man-made end to the fetus's natural course of development. Thus, by the lights of traditional Catholic thinking, abortion is wrong because it disrupts natural processes. This type of argument, however, can hardly show that Christians "must" oppose abortion. The argument depends on natural-law theory, and, as we have seen, natural-law theory is based on a worldview that predates modern science. Christians today need not reject modern science—the Pope himself, for example, believes in Charles Darwin's 19th-century theory of evolution as well as the 20th-century idea that the universe began with a "Big Bang." Thus, Christians are not required to oppose abortion based on natural-law considerations.

At any rate, to say that abortion disrupts a natural process is to say nothing about the moral status of the fetus. The Pope does not merely believe that abortion is immoral, like using a condom; he believes that abortion is *murder*. How did this position become dominant within the Catholic Church? Have Church leaders always regarded the fetus as enjoying a special moral status?

For most of the Church's history—until around A.D. 1200—little of relevance is known. Back then, there were no universities, and the Church was not especially intellectual. People believed all kinds of things, for all kinds of reasons. But in the 13th century, Saint Thomas Aquinas constructed a philosophical system that became the bedrock of later Catholic thought. The key question, Aquinas believed, is whether the fetus has a soul: if it does, then abortion is murder; if it doesn't, then abortion is not murder. Does the fetus have a soul? Aquinas accepted Aristotle's idea that the soul is the "substantial form" of man. Let's not worry about exactly what that means; what's important is that human beings are supposed to acquire a "substantial form" only when their bodies take on human shape. So now the key question is: When do human beings first look human?

When a baby is born, anyone can see that it has a human shape. In Aquinas's day, however, nobody knew when fetuses begin to look human—after all, fetal development occurs in the mother's womb, out of sight. Aristotle had believed, for no good reason, that males acquire a soul 40 days after conception and females do after 90 days. Presumably, many Christians accepted his view. At any rate, for the next several centuries, it was natural for Catholics to strongly oppose abortion at any stage of pregnancy, because the fetus *might* have already acquired a human form, and so abortion *might* be murder.

Contrary to popular belief, the Catholic Church has never officially maintained that the fetus acquires a soul at the moment of conception. Around 1600, however, some theologians began to say that the soul enters the body a few days after conception, and so abortion is murder even at an early stage. This monumentally important change in Catholic thinking occurred without extended theological debate. Perhaps it seemed unimportant because the Church already opposed early-term abortions. Yet we understand little about why the Church changed its position.

Today we know a lot about fetal development. We know, through microscopes and ultrasounds, that fetuses do not look human until several weeks into the pregnancy. Thus, a follower of Aquinas should now say that fetuses do not have a soul during the first month or two of pregnancy. However, there has been no movement inside the Catholic Church to adopt that position. For reasons that remain murky, the Church adopted a conservative view of the status of the fetus in the 1600s, and it has held fast to that view ever since.

The purpose of reviewing this history is not to suggest that the contemporary church's position is wrong. For all I have said, it may be right. My point, rather, is this: every generation interprets its traditions to support its favored moral views. Abortion is but one example of this. We could also have discussed the church's shifting views on slavery, or the status of women, or capital punishment. In each case, the moral stance taken by the Church seems not to be derived from the Bible so much as imposed on it.

The arguments in this chapter point to a common conclusion: Right and wrong are not to be understood in terms of God's will; morality is a matter of reason and conscience, not religious faith; and in any case, religious considerations do not provide definitive solutions to most of the moral problems that we face. Morality and religion are, in a word, different. Of course, religious beliefs do sometimes bear on moral issues. Consider, for example, the doctrine of eternal life. If some people go to heaven when they die—so that dying is a good thing for them—then this might affect the morality of killing these people. Or suppose we believe, upon studying ancient prophecies, that the world is about to end. This might diminish our fear of climate change. The relationship between morality and religion is complicated, but it is a relationship between two different subjects.

This conclusion may strike some readers as antireligious. However, it has not been reached by questioning the validity of religion. The arguments we have considered do not assume that Christianity or any other theological system is false; they merely show that, even if such a system is true, morality remains an independent matter.

CHAPTER 5

*E*thical Egoism

The achievement of his own happiness is man's highest moral purpose.

AYN RAND, THE VIRTUE OF SELFISHNESS (1961)

5.1. Is There a Duty to Help the Starving?

Each year millions of people die from health problems brought on by malnutrition. Often, those who die are children. Every day, around 22,000 children under the age of 5 die, almost always from preventable causes. That comes to over 8 million deaths each year. Even if this estimate is too high, the number who die is staggering.

Poverty poses an acute problem for many of us who are not poor. We spend money on ourselves, not only on necessities but on luxuries—DVDs, jewelry, concert tickets, iPods, and so on. In America, even people with modest incomes enjoy such things. But we could forgo our luxuries and give the money for famine relief instead. The fact that we don't suggests that we regard our luxuries as more important than the lives of the starving.

Why do we let people starve when we could save them? Few of us actually believe our luxuries are that important. Most of us, if asked the question directly, would probably be a bit embarrassed, and we might say we should do more to help. One reason we don't do more is that we rarely think about the problem. Living our own comfortable lives, we are insulated from it. The starving people are dying at some distance from us; we do not see them, and we can avoid even thinking about them. When we do think of them, it is only abstractly, as statistics. Unfortunately for the hungry, statistics have little power to move us.

We respond differently when there is a "crisis," as when an earthquake struck Japan in 2011, killing thousands, triggering a tsunami, and causing meltdowns at several nuclear power plants. Then the crisis is big news and relief efforts are mobilized. But when the needy are scattered, the situation does not seem so pressing. The 8 million children who die every year would probably be saved if they were all gathered in, say, Chicago.

But leaving aside the question of why we behave as we do, what is our duty? What *should* we do? Common sense might tell us to balance our own interests against the interests of others. It is understandable, of course, that we look out for ourselves, and people cannot be blamed for attending to their own basic needs. But at the same time, the needs of others are important, and when we can help others—especially at little cost to ourselves—we should do so. So, if you have an extra $10, and giving it to charity would help save a child's life, then common-sense morality would say that you should do so.

This way of thinking assumes that we have duties to others simply because *they are people who could be helped or harmed by what we do*. If a certain action would benefit (or harm) other people, then that is a reason why we should (or should not) perform that action. The commonsense assumption is that other people's interests *count*, from a moral point of view.

But one person's common sense is another person's naïve platitude. Some people believe that we have no duties to others. On their view, known as Ethical Egoism, each person ought to pursue his or her own self-interest exclusively. This is the morality of selfishness. It holds that our only duty is to do what is best for ourselves. Other people matter only insofar as they can benefit us.

5.2. Psychological Egoism

Before we discuss Ethical Egoism, we should discuss a theory it is often confused with—Psychological Egoism. Ethical Egoism claims that each person *ought* to pursue his or her own self-interest exclusively. Psychological Egoism, by contrast, asserts that each person *does in fact* pursue his or her own self-interest exclusively. Thus, these theories are very different. It is one thing to say that people are self-interested and that our neighbors will not give to charity. It is quite another thing to say that people *ought* to be self-interested and that our neighbors *ought* not to give to charity. Psychological Egoism makes a claim about human nature, or about the way things are; Ethical Egoism makes a claim about morality, or about the way things should be.

Psychological Egoism is not a theory of ethics; rather, it is a theory of human psychology. But ethicists have always worried about it. If Psychological Egoism were true, then moral philosophy itself would seem pointless. After all, if people are going to behave selfishly *no matter what,* then what's the point of discussing what they "ought" to do? Whatever it is they "ought" to do, they aren't going to do it. It might be naïve of us to think that our moral theories can matter in the real world.

Is Altruism Possible? When World War II began, Raoul Wallenberg was an unknown businessman living in Sweden. Sweden was a good place to be during the war. As a neutral country, it was never bombed, blockaded, or invaded. Yet, in 1944, Wallenberg voluntarily left Sweden for Nazi-controlled Hungary. Officially, Wallenberg was going to be just another Swedish diplomat in Budapest. However, his real mission was to save lives. In Hungary, Hitler had begun implementing his "final solution to the Jewish problem": Jews were being rounded up, deported, and then murdered at Nazi killing stations. Wallenberg wanted to stop the slaughter.

Wallenberg did help to persuade the Hungarian government to halt the deportations. However, the Hungarian government was soon replaced by a Nazi puppet regime, and the mass killing resumed. Wallenberg then issued "Swedish Protective Passes" to thousands of Jews, insisting that they all had connections to Sweden and were under the protection of his government. Wallenberg helped many people hide. When they were discovered, he would stand between them and the Nazis, telling the Germans that they would have to shoot him first. Wallenberg saved thousands of human lives. At the end of the war, when chaos prevailed, he stayed behind as other diplomats fled. After the war, Wallenberg disappeared, and for a long time his fate was unknown. Now we believe that he was killed, not by the Germans, but by the Soviets, who imprisoned him after taking over Hungary.

Wallenberg's story is especially dramatic, but it is not unique. The Israeli government recognizes over 22,000 Gentiles who risked their lives trying to save Jews from being murdered in the Holocaust. The Israelis call these women and men "The Righteous among the Nations." And though few of us have saved lives, acts of altruism appear to be common. People do favors for one another. They give blood. They build homeless shelters. They volunteer in hospitals. They read to the blind. Many people give money to worthy causes. In some cases, the amount given is extraordinary. Warren Buffett, an American businessman, gave $37 billion to the Bill and Melinda Gates Foundation to promote global health and education. Zell Kravinsky, an American real estate investor, gave his entire $45-million fortune to charity. And then, for good measure, Kravinsky donated one of his kidneys to a complete stranger. Oseola McCarty, an 87-year-old African-American woman from Hattiesburg, Mississippi, gave $150,000 to endow a scholarship fund at the University of Southern Mississippi. For 75 years, she had saved up money, working as a maid. She never owned a car, and at the age of 87 she still walked over a mile to the nearest grocery store, pushing her own shopping cart.

These are remarkable deeds, but should they be taken at face value? According to Psychological Egoism, we may believe ourselves to be noble and self-sacrificing, but that is only an illusion. In reality, we care only for ourselves. Could this theory be true? Why have people believed it, in the face of so much evidence to the contrary? Two arguments are often given for Psychological Egoism.

The Argument That We Always Do What We Want to Do. "Every act you have ever performed since the day you were born was performed because you wanted something." So wrote Dale Carnegie, author of the first and best self-help book, *How to Win Friends and Influence People* (1936). Carnegie thought of desire as the key to human psychology. Thus, when we describe one person's action as altruistic and another person's action as self-interested, we may be overlooking the fact that in each case *the person is merely doing what he or she most wants to do.* For example, if Raoul Wallenberg chose to go to Hungary, then he wanted to go there more than he wanted to remain in Sweden—and why should he be praised for altruism when he was only doing what he wanted to do? His action sprang from his own desires, from his own sense of what he wanted. Thus, he was moved by his own self-interest. And because the same may be said about any alleged act of kindness, we can conclude that Psychological Egoism must be true.

This argument, however, is flawed. There are things that we do, not because we want to, but because we feel that we *ought* to. For example, I may write my grandmother a letter because I promised my mother I would, even though I don't want to do it. It is sometimes suggested that we do such things because we most want to keep our promises. But that is not true. It is simply false to say that my strongest desire is to keep my promise. What I most want is to break my promise, but I don't, as a matter of conscience. For all we know, Wallenberg was in this position: Perhaps he wanted to stay in Sweden, but he felt that he had to go to Hungary to save lives. In any case, the fact that he chose to go does not imply that he most wanted to do so.

The argument has a second flaw. Suppose we concede that we always act on our strongest desires. Even if this were so, it would not follow that Wallenberg acted out of self-interest. For if Wallenberg wanted to help others, even at great risk to himself, then that is precisely what makes his behavior contrary to Psychological Egoism. The mere fact that you act on your own desires does not mean that you are looking out for yourself; it all depends on *what* you desire. If you care only about yourself and give no thought to others, then you are acting out of self-interest; but if you want other people to be happy, and you act on that desire, then you are not. To put the point another way: In assessing whether an action is self-interested, the issue is not *whether* the action is based on a desire; the issue is *what kind of desire it is based on.* If you want to help someone else, then your motive is altruistic, not self-interested.

Therefore, this argument goes wrong in just about every way that an argument can go wrong: The premise is not true—we don't always do what we most want to do—and even if it were true, the conclusion would not follow from it.

The Argument That We Always Do What Makes Us Feel Good. The second argument for Psychological Egoism appeals to the fact that so-called altruistic actions produce a sense of self-satisfaction in the person who performs them. Acting "unselfishly" makes people feel good about themselves, and that is the real point of it.

According to a 19th-century newspaper, this argument was made by Abraham Lincoln. The Springfield, Illinois, *Monitor* reported:

> Mr. Lincoln once remarked to a fellow-passenger on an old-time mud coach that all men were prompted by selfishness in doing good. His fellow-passenger was antagonizing this position when they were passing over a corduroy bridge that spanned a slough. As they crossed this bridge they espied an old razor-backed sow on the bank making a terrible noise because her pigs had got into the slough and were in danger of drowning. As the old coach began to climb the hill, Mr. Lincoln called out, "Driver, can't you stop just a moment?" Then Mr. Lincoln jumped out, ran back, and lifted the little pigs out of the mud and water and placed them on the bank. When he returned, his companion remarked: "Now, Abe, where does selfishness come in on this little episode?" "Why, bless your soul, Ed, that was the very essence of selfishness. I should have had no peace of mind all day had I gone on and left that suffering old sow worrying over those pigs. I did it to get peace of mind, don't you see?"

In this story, Honest Abe employs a time-honored tactic of Psychological Egoism: *the strategy of reinterpreting motives.* Everyone knows that people sometimes seem to act altruistically; but if we look deeper, we may find that something else is going on. And usually it is not hard to discover that the "unselfish" behavior is actually connected to some benefit for the person who does it. Thus, Lincoln talks about the peace of mind he got from rescuing the pigs.

Other examples of alleged altruism can also be reinterpreted. According to some of Raoul Wallenberg's friends, before traveling to Hungary he was depressed and unhappy that his life wasn't amounting to much. So he undertook deeds that would make him a heroic figure. His quest for a more significant life was spectacularly successful—here we are, more than 60 years after his death, talking about him. Mother Teresa, the nun who spent her life working among the poor in Calcutta, is often cited as a perfect example of altruism—but, of course, she believed that she would be handsomely rewarded in heaven. And as for Zell Kravinsky, who gave away both his fortune and a kidney, his parents never gave him much praise, so he was always trying to do things that even they would admire. Kravinsky himself said that, as he began to give away his money, he came to think of a donation as "a treat to myself. I really thought of it as something pleasurable."

Despite all this, Lincoln's argument is badly flawed. It may be true that one of Lincoln's motives in saving the pigs was to preserve his own peace of mind. *But the fact that Lincoln had a self-interested motive doesn't mean that he didn't have benevolent motives as well.* In fact, Lincoln's desire to help the pigs might have been even greater than his desire to preserve his peace of mind. And if this isn't true in Lincoln's case, it will be true in other cases: If I see a child drowning, my desire to help that child will usually be greater than my desire to avoid a guilty conscience. Cases like these are counterexamples to Psychological Egoism.

In some instances of altruism, we may have *no* self-interested motives. For example, in 2007, a 50-year-old construction worker named Wesley Autrey was waiting for a subway train in New York City. Autrey saw a man near him collapse, his body convulsing. The man got up, only to stumble to the edge of the platform and fall onto the train tracks. At that moment, the headlights of a train appeared. "I had to make a split[-second] decision," Autrey later said. He then leapt onto the tracks and lay on top of the man, pressing him down into a space a foot deep. The train's brakes screeched, but it could not stop in time. People on the platform screamed. Five cars passed over the men, smudging Autrey's blue knit cap with grease. When onlookers realized that both men were safe, they broke out into applause. "I just saw someone who needed help," Autrey later said. He had saved the man's life, never giving a thought to his own well-being.

There is a general lesson to be learned here, having to do with the nature of desire. We want all sorts of things—money, friends, fame, a new car, and so on—and because we desire these things, we may derive satisfaction from getting them. But the object of our desire is typically *not* the feeling of satisfaction—that is not what we are after. What we want is simply the money, the friends, the fame, and the car. It is the same with helping others. Our desire to help others often comes first; the good feelings we may get are merely a by-product.

Conclusion about Psychological Egoism. If Psychological Egoism is so implausible, why have so many intelligent people been attracted to it? Some people like the theory's cynical view of human nature. Others may like its simplicity. And, indeed, it would be pleasing if a single factor could explain all human behavior. But human beings seem to be too complicated for that. Psychological Egoism is not a credible theory.

Thus, morality has nothing to fear from Psychological Egoism. Given that we *can* be moved by regard for others, it is not pointless to talk about whether we *should* help our neighbors. Moral theorizing need not be a naïve endeavor, based on an unrealistic view of human nature.

5.3. Three Arguments for Ethical Egoism

Ethical Egoism, again, is the doctrine that each person ought to pursue his or her own self-interest exclusively. This is not the commonsense idea that one should promote one's own interests *in addition to* the interests of others. Ethical Egoism is the radical idea that the principle of self-interest accounts for *all* of one's obligations.

However, Ethical Egoism does not tell you to *avoid* helping others. Sometimes your interests will coincide with the well-being of others, so by helping yourself you'll help them too. For example, if you can convince your teacher to cancel the assignment, this will benefit you *and* your classmates. Ethical Egoism does not forbid such actions; in fact, it may recommend them. The theory insists only that in such cases the benefit to others is not what makes the act right. Rather, the act is right because it is to your own advantage.

Nor does Ethical Egoism imply that in pursuing your interests, you should always do what you want to, or what offers you the most short-term pleasure. Someone may want to smoke cigarettes, or bet all his money at the racetrack, or set up a meth lab in his basement. Ethical Egoism would frown on all this, despite the short-term benefits. Ethical Egoism says that a person ought to do what really is in his or her own best interests, over the long run. It endorses selfishness, not foolishness.

Now let's discuss the three main arguments for Ethical Egoism.

The Argument That Altruism Is Self-Defeating. The first argument has several variations:

- Each of us is intimately familiar with our own individual wants and needs. Moreover, each of us is uniquely placed to pursue those wants and needs effectively. At the same time, we understand the desires and needs of other people only imperfectly, and we are not well situated to pursue them. Therefore, if we try to be "our brother's keeper," we will often bungle the job and end up doing more harm than good.
- At the same time, the policy of "looking out for others" is an offensive intrusion into other people's privacy; it is essentially a policy of minding other people's business.
- Making other people the object of one's "charity" is degrading to them; it robs them of their dignity and self-respect. The offer of charity says, in effect, that they are not competent to care for themselves; and the statement is self-fulfilling. They cease to be self-reliant and become passively dependent on others. That is why the recipients of "charity" are often resentful rather than appreciative.

In each case, the policy of "looking out for others" is said to be self-defeating. If we want to do what is best for people, we should not adopt so-called altruistic policies. On the contrary, if each person looks after his or her own interests, everyone will be better off.

It is possible to object to this argument on a number of grounds. Of course, no one favors bungling, butting in, or depriving people of their self-respect. But is that really what's going on when we feed hungry children? Is the starving child in Niger really harmed when we "intrude" into "her business" by giving her food? It hardly seems likely. Yet we can set this point aside, for this way of thinking has an even more serious defect.

The trouble is that it isn't really an argument for Ethical Egoism at all. The argument concludes that we should adopt certain policies of behavior, and on the surface, they appear to be egoistic policies. However, the *reason* we should adopt those policies is decidedly unegoistic. It is said that adopting those policies will promote the betterment of society—but according to Ethical Egoism, that is not something we should care about. Spelled out fully, the argument says:

(1) We ought to do whatever will best promote everyone's interests.

(2) The best way to promote everyone's interests is for each of us to pursue our own interests exclusively.

(3) Therefore, each of us should pursue our own interests exclusively.

If we accept this reasoning, then we are not Ethical Egoists. Even though we might behave like egoists, our ultimate principle is one of beneficence—we are trying to help everyone, and not just ourselves. Rather than being egoists, we turn out to be altruists with a peculiar view of what promotes the general welfare.

Ayn Rand's Argument. Ayn Rand (1905–1982) is not read much by philosophers. The ideas associated with her name—that capitalism is a morally superior economic system and that morality demands absolute respect for the rights of individuals—are developed more rigorously by other writers. Nevertheless, she was a charismatic figure who attracted a devoted following during her lifetime. Today, roughly 30 years after her death, the Ayn Rand industry is still going strong. Ethical Egoism is associated with her more than with any other 20th-century writer.

Ayn Rand regarded the "ethics of altruism" as a totally destructive idea, both in society as a whole and in the lives of those taken in by it. Altruism, to her way of thinking, leads to a denial of the value of the individual. It says to a person: Your life is merely something to be sacrificed. "If a man accepts the ethics of altruism," she writes, "his first concern is not how to live his life, but how to sacrifice it." Those who promote the ethics of altruism are beneath contempt—they are parasites who, rather than working to build and sustain their own lives, leech off those who do. Rand continues:

> Parasites, moochers, looters, brutes and thugs can be of no value to a human being—nor can he gain any benefit from living in a society geared to *their* needs, demands and protections, a society that treats him as a sacrificial animal and penalizes him for his virtues in order to reward *them* for their vices, which means: a society based on the ethics of altruism.

By "sacrificing one's life," Rand does not mean anything so dramatic as dying. A person's life consists, in part, of projects undertaken and goods earned and created. Thus, to demand that a person abandon his projects or give up his goods is to demand that he "sacrifice his life."

Rand also suggests that there is a metaphysical basis for Ethical Egoism. Somehow, it is the only ethic that takes seriously the *reality* of the individual person. She bemoans "the enormity of the extent to which altruism erodes men's capacity to grasp . . . the value of an individual life; it reveals a mind from which the reality of a human being has been wiped out."

What, then, of the hungry children? It might be said that Ethical Egoism itself "reveals a mind from which the reality of a human being has been wiped out," namely, the human being who is starving. But Rand quotes with approval the answer given by one of her followers: "Once, when Barbara Brandon was asked by a student: 'What will happen to the poor . . . ?' she answered: 'If *you* want to help them, you will not be stopped.'"

All these remarks are part of one continuous argument that goes something like this:

(1) Each person has only one life to live. If we value the individual, then we must agree that this life is of supreme importance. After all, it is all one has, and all one is.

(2) The ethics of altruism regards the life of the individual as something that may be sacrificed for the good of others. Therefore, the ethics of altruism does not take seriously the value of the individual.

(3) Ethical Egoism, which allows each person to view his or her own life as being of ultimate value, does take the individual seriously—it is, in fact, the only philosophy that does.

(4) Thus, Ethical Egoism is the philosophy that we ought to accept.

One problem with this argument, as you may have noticed, is that it assumes we have only two options: Either we accept the ethics of altruism, or we accept Ethical Egoism. The choice is then made to look obvious by depicting the ethics of altruism as an insane doctrine that only an idiot would accept. The ethics of altruism is said to be the view that one's own interests have *no* value and that one must be ready to sacrifice oneself *totally* whenever *anybody* asks it. If this is the alternative, then any other view, including Ethical Egoism, will look good by comparison.

But that is hardly a fair picture of the options. What we called the commonsense view stands between the two extremes. It says that one's own interests and the interests of others are *both* important, and must be balanced against each other. Sometimes, one should act in the interests of others; other times, one should take care of oneself. So, even if we should reject the extreme ethics of altruism, it does not follow that we must accept the other extreme of Ethical Egoism. There is a middle ground.

Ethical Egoism as Compatible with Commonsense Morality. The third argument takes a different approach. Ethical Egoism is usually presented as a *revisionist* moral philosophy, that is, as a philosophy that says our commonsense moral views are mistaken. It is possible, however, to interpret Ethical Egoism as a theory that accepts commonsense morality.

This interpretation goes as follows: Ordinary morality consists in obeying certain rules. We must speak the truth, keep our promises, avoid harming others, and so on. At first glance, these duties appear to have little in common—they are just a bunch of discrete rules. Yet there may be a unity to them. Ethical Egoists would say that all these duties are ultimately derived from the one fundamental principle of self-interest.

Understood in this way, Ethical Egoism is not such a radical doctrine. It does not challenge commonsense morality; it only tries to explain and systematize it. And it does a surprisingly good job. It can provide plausible explanations of the duties mentioned above, and more:

- *The duty not to harm others:* If we do things that harm other people, other people will not mind doing things that harm us. We will be shunned and despised; others will not be our friends and will not help us out when we need it. If our offenses are serious enough, we may end up in jail. Thus, it is to our own advantage to avoid harming others.

- *The duty not to lie:* If we lie to other people, we will suffer all the ill effects of a bad reputation. People will distrust us and avoid doing business with us. People will be dishonest with us once they realize that we have been dishonest with them. Thus, it is to our own advantage to be truthful.
- *The duty to keep our promises:* It is to our own advantage to enter into mutually beneficial arrangements with other people. To benefit from those arrangements, we need to be able to rely on others to keep their word. But we can hardly expect them to do that if we do not keep our promises to them. Therefore, from the point of view of self-interest, we should keep our promises.

Pursuing this line of reasoning, Thomas Hobbes (1588–1679) suggested that the principle of Ethical Egoism leads to nothing less than the Golden Rule: We should "do unto others" because if we do, others will be more likely to "do unto us."

Does this argument succeed in establishing Ethical Egoism as a viable theory of morality? It may be the best try. However, there are two serious problems with it. First, the argument does not prove as much as it needs to. It shows only that it is *mostly* to one's advantage to tell the truth, to keep one's promises, and to avoid harming others. But a situation might arise in which you could profit from doing something horrible, like killing someone. In such a case, Ethical Egoism cannot explain why you shouldn't do the horrible thing. Thus, it looks like some of our moral obligations cannot be derived from self-interest.

Second, suppose it is true that giving money to famine relief is somehow to one's own advantage. It doesn't follow that this is the *only* reason to do so. Another reason might be *to help the starving people.* Ethical Egoism says that self-interest is the only reason to help others, but nothing in the present argument really supports that.

5.4. Three Arguments against Ethical Egoism

The Argument That Ethical Egoism Endorses Wickedness. Consider these wicked actions, taken from various newspaper stories: To make more money, a pharmacist filled prescriptions for cancer patients using watered-down drugs. A paramedic gave emergency patients injections of sterile water rather than morphine, so he could sell the morphine. Parents fed a baby acid so they could fake a lawsuit, claiming the baby's formula was tainted. A nurse raped two patients while they were unconscious. A 73-year-old man kept his daughter locked in a cellar for 24 years and fathered seven children with her, against her will. A 60-year-old man shot his letter carrier seven times because he was $90,000 in debt and thought that being in federal prison would be better than being homeless.

Suppose that someone could actually benefit by doing such things. Wouldn't Ethical Egoism have to approve of such actions? This seems like enough to discredit the doctrine. However, this objection might be unfair to Ethical Egoism, because in saying that these actions are wicked, it assumes a nonegoistic conception of wickedness. Thus, some philosophers have tried to show that there are deeper logical problems with Ethical Egoism. The following argument is typical of such proposals.

The Argument That Ethical Egoism Is Logically Inconsistent. In his book *The Moral Point of View* (1958), Kurt Baier argues that Ethical Egoism cannot be correct, on purely logical grounds. Baier thinks that the theory leads to contradictions. If this is true, then Ethical Egoism is indeed mistaken, for no theory can be true if it contradicts itself.

Suppose, Baier says, two people are running for president. Let's call them "D" and "R," to stand for "Democrat" and "Republican." Because it would be in D's interest to win, it would be in D's interest to kill R. From this it follows, on Ethical Egoism, that D ought to kill R—it is D's moral duty to do so. But it is also true that it is in R's interest to stay alive. From this it follows that R ought to stop D from killing her—that is R's duty. Now here's the problem. When R protects herself from D, her act is both wrong and not wrong—wrong because it prevents D from doing his duty, and not wrong because it is in R's best interests. But one and the same act cannot be both morally wrong and not morally wrong.

Does this argument refute Ethical Egoism? At first glance, it seems persuasive. However, it is complicated, so we need to set it out with each step individually identified. Then we will be in a better position to evaluate it. Spelled out fully, it goes like this:

(1) Suppose it is each person's duty to do what is in his own best interest.

(2) It is in D's best interest to kill R so that D will win the election.

(3) It is in R's best interest to prevent D from killing her.

(4) Therefore, D's duty is to kill R, and R's duty is to prevent D from doing it.

(5) But it is wrong to prevent someone from doing his duty.

(6) Therefore, it is wrong for R to prevent D from killing her.

(7) Therefore, it is both wrong and not wrong for R to prevent D from killing her.

(8) But no act can be wrong and not wrong; that is a contradiction.

(9) Therefore, the assumption with which we started—that it is each person's duty to do what is in his own best interest—cannot be true.

When the argument is set out in this way, we can see its hidden flaw. The logical contradiction—that it is wrong and not wrong for R to prevent D from killing her—does not follow simply from the principle of Ethical Egoism as stated in step (1). It follows from that principle *together with* the premise expressed in step (5), namely, that "it is wrong to prevent someone from doing his duty." By putting step (5) in the argument, Baier has added his own assumption.

Thus, we need not reject Ethical Egoism. Instead, we could simply reject this additional premise and thereby avoid the contradiction. That is surely what the Ethical Egoist would do, for the Ethical Egoist would never say, without qualification, that it is always wrong to prevent someone from doing his duty. He would say, instead, that whether one ought to prevent someone from doing his duty depends entirely on whether it would be to one's own advantage to do so. Regardless of whether we like this idea, it is at least what the Ethical Egoist would say. And so, this attempt to convict the egoist of self-contradiction fails.

The Argument That Ethical Egoism Is Unacceptably Arbitrary.
This argument may refute Ethical Egoism. It is at least the deepest of the arguments we'll consider, because it tries to explain
why the interests of other people *should* matter to us. But before
presenting this argument, we need to look at a general point
about moral values.

There is a whole family of moral views that have this in common: They divide people into groups and say that the interests
of some groups count more than the interests of other groups.
Racism is the most conspicuous example. Racists divide people
into groups according to race and assign greater importance
to the well-being of one race than to the well-being of other
races. All forms of discrimination work like this—anti-Semitism,
nationalism, sexism, ageism, and so on. People in the sway of
such attitudes will think, in effect, "*My* race counts for more,"
or "Those who believe in *my* religion count for more," or "*My*
country counts for more," and so on.

Can such ideas be defended? The people who accept such
views don't usually give arguments for them—racists, for example, rarely try to offer a rational justification for racism. But
suppose they did. What could they say?

There is a general principle that stands in the way of any
such justification. Let's call it the Principle of Equal Treatment:
*We should treat people in the same way unless there is a good reason
not to.* For example, suppose we're considering whether to
admit two students to law school. If both students graduated
from college with honors and aced the entrance exam—if both
are equally qualified—then it is merely arbitrary to admit one
but not the other. However, if one graduated with honors and
scored well on the admissions test while the other dropped out
of college and never took the test, then it is acceptable to admit
the first student but not the second.

At root, the Principle of Equal Treatment is a principle
that requires fairness in our dealings with others: like cases
should be treated alike, and only unlike cases may be treated
differently. Two points should be made about the principle.
The first is that treating people in the same way does not always
mean ensuring the same outcome for them. During the Viet-
nam War, young American men desperately wanted to avoid
getting drafted into the armed services, and the government
had to decide the order in which draft boards would call people

up. In 1969, the first "draft lottery" was televised to a national audience. Here is how it worked: The days of the year were written on 366 slips of paper (one slip for February 29) and inserted into blue plastic capsules. Those capsules were placed in a glass jar and mixed up. Then, one by one, the capsules were drawn. The first was for September 14—young men with that birthday, age 18–26, would be drafted first. The winners of the lottery, drawn last, were born on June 8. These young men never got drafted. In college dormitories, groups of students watched the drawings live, and it was easy to tell whose birthday had just come up—whoever just groaned or swore. Obviously, the outcomes were different: In the end, some people got drafted and others didn't. However, the process was fair. By giving everyone an equal chance in the lottery, the government treated everyone in the same way.

A second point concerns the *scope* of the principle, or what situations it applies to. Suppose you're not going to use your ticket to the big game, so you give it to a friend. In doing so, you are treating your friend better than everyone else you could have given the ticket to. Does your action violate the Principle of Equal Treatment? Does it need justification? Moral philosophers disagree on this question. Some think that the principle does not apply to cases like this. The principle applies only in "moral contexts," and what you should do with your ticket is not important enough to count as a moral question. Others think that your action does require justification, and various justifications might be offered. Your action might be justified by the nature of friendship; or by the fact that it would be impossible for you to hold a lottery at the last minute for all the ticketless fans; or by the fact that you own the ticket, so you can do what you want with it. It doesn't matter, from our point of view, whether the Principle of Equal Treatment applies only in so-called "moral contexts." Suffice it to say that everyone accepts the principle, under one interpretation or another. Everyone believes in treating people similarly, unless the facts demand otherwise.

Let's now apply that principle to racism. Can a racist point to any differences between, say, white people and black people that would justify treating them differently? In the past, racists have sometimes tried to do this by portraying blacks as lazy, unintelligent, and threatening. In doing so, the racists show that even they accept the Principle of Equal Treatment—the point of such stereotypes is to supply the "good reasons" needed to justify differences in treatment. If such accusations were true, then differential treatment would be justified in some circumstances. But, of course, they are not true; there are no such differences between the races. Thus, racism is an arbitrary doctrine—it advocates treating people differently even though there are no good reasons to do so.

Ethical Egoism is a moral theory of the same type. It advocates dividing the world into two categories of people—ourselves and everyone else—and it urges us to regard the interests of those in the first group as more important than the interests of those in the second group. But each of us can ask, What is the difference between me and everyone else that justifies placing myself in this special category? Am I more intelligent? Are my accomplishments greater? Do I enjoy life more? Are my needs and abilities different from the needs and abilities of others? In short, *what makes me so special?* Failing an answer, it turns out that Ethical Egoism is an arbitrary doctrine, in the same way that racism is arbitrary. Both doctrines violate the Principle of Equal Treatment.

Thus, we should care about the interests of other people because their needs and desires are comparable to our own. Consider, one last time, the starving children we could feed by giving up some of our luxuries. Why should we care about them? We care about ourselves, of course—if we were starving, we would do almost anything to get food. But what is the difference between us and them? Does hunger affect them any less? Are they less deserving than we are? If we can find no relevant difference between us and them, then we must admit that, if our needs should be met, then so should theirs. This realization—that we are on a par with one another—is the deepest reason why our morality must recognize the needs of others. And that is why, ultimately, Ethical Egoism fails as a moral theory.

CHAPTER 6

The Social Contract Theory

Wherever law ends, tyranny begins . . .
JOHN LOCKE, *THE SECOND TREATISE OF GOVERNMENT* (1690)

6.1. Hobbes's Argument

Suppose we take away all the traditional props for morality. Assume, first, that there is no God to issue commands and reward virtue. Next, suppose that there are no "natural purposes"—objects in nature have no inherent functions or intended uses. Finally, assume that human beings are naturally selfish. Where, then, could morality come from? If we cannot appeal to God, natural purpose, or altruism, is there anything left to base morality on?

Thomas Hobbes, the leading British philosopher of the 17th century, tried to show that morality does not depend on any of those things. Instead, morality should be understood as the solution to a practical problem that arises for self-interested human beings. We all want to live as well as possible; but in order to flourish, we need a peaceful, cooperative social order. And we cannot have one without rules. Those rules *are* the moral rules; morality consists of the precepts we need to follow in order to get the benefits of social living. That—not God, inherent purposes, or altruism—is the key to understanding ethics.

Hobbes begins by asking what it would be like if there were no way to enforce social rules. Suppose there were no government institutions—no laws, no police, and no courts. In this situation, each of us would be free to do as we pleased. Hobbes called this "the state of nature." What would it be like? Hobbes thought it would be dreadful. In the state of nature, he says,

> there would be no place for industry, because the fruit thereof is uncertain: and consequently no culture of

the earth; no navigation, nor use of the commodities that may be imported by sea; no commodious building; no instruments of moving, and removing, such things as require much force; no knowledge of the face of the earth; no account of time; no arts; no letters; no society; and which is worst of all, continual fear, and danger of violent death; and the life of man, solitary, poor, nasty, brutish, and short.

The state of nature would be awful, Hobbes thought, due to four basic facts about human life:

- There is *equality of need*. Each of us needs the same basic things in order to survive—food, clothing, shelter, and so on. Although we may differ in some of our needs (diabetics need insulin, others don't), we are all essentially alike.
- There is *scarcity*. We do not live in the Garden of Eden, where milk flows in streams and every tree hangs heavy with fruit. The world is a hard, inhospitable place, where the things we need do not come in abundance. We have to work hard to produce them, and even then they may be in short supply.
- There is *the essential equality of human power*. Who will get the scarce goods? No one can simply take what she wants. Even though some people are smarter and tougher than others, even the strongest can be brought down when those who are less strong act together.
- Finally, there is *limited altruism*. If we cannot prevail by our own strength, what hope do we have? Can we rely on the goodwill of others? We cannot. Even if people are not wholly selfish, they care most about themselves, and we cannot assume that they will step aside when their interests conflict with ours.

Together, these facts paint a grim picture. We all need the same basic things, and there aren't enough of them to go around. Therefore, we will have to compete for them. But no one can prevail in this competition, and no one—or almost no one—will look after the needs of his neighbors. The result, as Hobbes puts it, is a "constant state of war, of one with all." And it is a war no one can win. Whoever wants to survive will try to seize what he needs and prepare to defend it from attack.

Meanwhile, others will be doing the same thing. Life in the state of nature would be intolerable.

Hobbes did not think this was mere speculation. He pointed out that this is what actually happens when governments collapse during civil uprisings. People hoard food, arm themselves, and lock out their neighbors. Moreover, nations themselves behave like this when international law is weak. Without a strong, overarching authority to maintain the peace, countries guard their borders, build up their armies, and feed their own people first.

To escape the state of nature, we must find a way to work together. In a stable and cooperative society, we can produce more essential goods and distribute them in a rational way. But establishing such a society is not easy. People must agree on rules to govern their interactions. They must agree, for example, not to harm one another and not to break their promises. Hobbes calls such an agreement "the social contract." As a society, we follow certain rules, and we have ways to enforce them. Some of those ways involve the law—if you assault someone, the police may arrest you. Other ways involve "the court of public opinion"—if you get a reputation for lying, then people may turn their backs on you. All of these rules, taken together, form the social contract.

It is only within the context of the social contract that we can become beneficent beings, because the contract creates the conditions under which we can afford to care about others. In the state of nature, it is every man for himself; it would be foolish for anyone to look out for others and put his own interests in jeopardy. But in society, altruism becomes possible. By releasing us from "the continual fear of violent death," the social contract frees us to take heed of others. Jean-Jacques Rousseau (1712–1778) went so far as to say that we become different kinds of creatures when we enter civilized relations with others. In *The Social Contract* (1762), he writes:

> The passage from the state of nature to the civil state produces a very remarkable change in man. . . . Then only, when the voice of duty takes the place of physical impulses . . . does man, who so far had considered only himself, find that he is forced to act on different principles, and to consult his reason before listening to his inclinations. . . . His faculties are so stimulated and

developed, . . . his feelings so ennobled, and his whole soul
so uplifted, that, did not the abuses of this new condition
often degrade him below that which he left, he would be
bound to bless continually the happy moment which took
him from it forever, and, instead of a stupid and unimagi-
native animal, made him an intelligent being and a man.

And what does the "voice of duty" require this new man
to do? It requires him to set aside his self-centered designs in
favor of rules that benefit everyone. But he is able to do this
only because others have agreed to do the same thing—that is
the essence of the "contract."

The Social Contract Theory explains the purpose of both
morality and government. The purpose of morality is to make
social living possible; the purpose of government is to enforce
vital moral rules. We can summarize the social contract conception of morality as follows: *Morality consists in the set of rules, governing behavior, that rational people will accept, on the condition that
others accept them as well.* And rational people will accept a rule
only if they can expect to gain from it. Thus, morality is about
mutual benefit; you and I are morally bound to follow a rule
only if we would be better off living in a society in which that
rule were usually followed.

6.2. The Prisoner's Dilemma

Hobbes's argument is one way of arriving at the Social Con-
tract Theory. Another argument makes use of the Prisoner's
Dilemma—a problem invented by Merrill M. Flood and Melvin
Dresher around 1950. Here's how the problem goes.

Suppose you live in a totalitarian society, and one day, to
your astonishment, you are arrested and charged with treason.
The police say that you have been plotting against the government with a man named Smith, who has also been arrested and
is being held in a separate cell. The interrogator demands that
you confess. You protest your innocence; you don't even know
Smith. But this does you no good. It soon becomes clear that
your captors are not interested in the truth; they merely want to
convict someone. They offer you the following deal:

- If Smith does not confess, but you confess and testify
  against him, then they will release you. You will go free,
  while Smith will be put away for 10 years.

- If Smith confesses and you do not, the situation will be reversed—he will go free while you get 10 years.
- If you both confess, you will each be sentenced to 5 years.
- If neither of you confesses, then there won't be enough evidence to convict either of you. They can hold you for a year, but then they will have to let both of you go.

Finally, you are told that Smith is being offered the same deal; but you cannot communicate with him, and you have no way of knowing what he will do.

The problem is this: Assuming that your only goal is to spend as little time in jail as possible, what should you do? Confess or not confess? For the purposes of this problem, you should forget about maintaining your dignity and standing up for your rights. That is not what this problem is about. You should also forget about trying to help Smith. This problem is strictly about calculating what is in your own best interests. What will get you free the quickest?

At first glance, it may seem that the question cannot be answered unless you know what Smith will do. But that is an illusion. The problem has a perfectly clear solution: No matter what Smith does, you should confess. This can be shown as follows:

(1) Either Smith will confess or he won't.

(2) Suppose Smith confesses. Then, if you confess you will get 5 years, whereas if you do not confess you will get 10 years. Therefore, if he confesses, you are better off confessing.

(3) On the other hand, suppose Smith does not confess. Then, if you confess you will go free, whereas if you do not confess you get one year. Therefore, if Smith does not confess, you will still be better off confessing.

(4) Therefore, you should confess. That will get you out of jail the soonest, no matter what Smith does.

So far, so good. But remember that Smith is being offered the same deal. Thus, he will also confess. The result will be that you both get 5-year sentences. *But if you had both done the opposite, you both could have gotten out in only one year.* It's a curious situation: Because you and Smith both act selfishly, you both wind up worse off.

Now suppose you can communicate with Smith. In that case, you could make a deal with him. You could agree that neither of you will confess; then you will both get the 1-year detention. By cooperating, you will both be better off than if you act independently. Cooperating will not get either of you the optimum result—immediate freedom—but it will get both of you a better result than you would have gotten alone.

It is vital, however, that any agreement between you and Smith be enforceable, because if he reneges and confesses while you keep the bargain, you will end up serving the maximum 10 years while he goes free. Thus, in order for you to rationally participate in such a deal, you need to be sure that Smith will keep up his end.

Morality as the Solution to Prisoner's-Dilemma-Type Problems.
The Prisoner's Dilemma is not just a clever puzzle. Although the story it tells is fictitious, the pattern it exemplifies comes up often in real life. Consider, for example, the choice between two general strategies of living. You could pursue your own interests exclusively—in every situation, you could do whatever will benefit yourself, taking no notice of anyone else. Let us call this "acting selfishly." Alternatively, you could care about others, balancing their interests against your own, and sometimes forgoing your own interests for their sake. Let us call this strategy "acting benevolently."

But it is not only you who has to decide how to live. Other people also have to choose which strategy to adopt. There are four possibilities: (a) You could be selfish while other people are benevolent; (b) others could be selfish while you are benevolent; (c) everyone could be selfish; and (d) everyone could be benevolent. How would you fare in each of these situations? Purely from the standpoint of your own welfare, you might assess the possibilities like this:

- You would be best off if you were selfish while other people were benevolent. You would get the benefit of their generosity without having to return the favor. (In this situation, you would be a "free rider.")
- Second-best would be if everyone were benevolent. You would no longer have the advantages that come from ignoring other people's interests, but you would be

treated well by others. (This is the situation of "ordinary morality.")

- A bad situation, but not the worst, would be one in which everyone was selfish. You would try to protect your own interests, but you would get little help from others. (This is Hobbes's "state of nature.")
- You would be worst off if you were benevolent while others were selfish. Other people could stab you in the back whenever they saw fit, but you would never do the same. You would come out on the short end every time. (This is the "sucker's payoff.")

This situation has the same structure as the Prisoner's Dilemma. In fact, it *is* a Prisoner's Dilemma, even though it involves no prisoners. Again, we can prove that you should adopt the selfish strategy:

(1) Either other people will respect your interests or they won't.

(2) If they do respect your interests, you will be better off not respecting theirs, at least whenever that would be to your advantage. This will be the optimum situation— you get to be a free rider.

(3) If they do not respect your interests, then it will be foolish for you to respect theirs. That will land you in the worst possible situation—you get the sucker's payoff.

(4) Therefore, regardless of what other people do, you are better off adopting the policy of looking out for yourself. You should be selfish.

And now we come to the catch: Other people, of course, can reason in the same way, and the result will be that we end up in Hobbes's state of nature. Everyone will be selfish, willing to knife anyone who gets in their way. In that situation, each of us would be worse off than if we all cooperated.

To escape the dilemma, we need another enforceable agreement, this time to obey the rules of mutually respectful social living. As before, cooperation will not yield the optimum outcome for each individual, but it will lead to a better result than noncooperation. We need, in David Gauthier's words, to "bargain our way into morality." We can do that by establishing laws and social customs that protect the interests of everyone involved.

6.3. Some Advantages of the Social Contract Theory

Morality, on this theory, consists in the rules that rational people will accept, on the condition that others accept them as well. The strength of this theory is due, in large part, to the fact that it provides plausible answers to some difficult questions.

1. *What moral rules are we bound to follow, and how are those rules justified?* The morally binding rules are the ones that facilitate harmonious social living. We could not live together in peace if we allowed murder, assault, theft, lying, promise breaking, and so on. The rules forbidding those acts are therefore justified by their tendency to promote harmony and cooperation. On the other hand, "moral rules" that condemn prostitution, sodomy, and sexual promiscuity cannot be justified on these grounds. How is social living hampered by private, voluntary sexual activity? How would it benefit us to agree to such rules? What people do behind closed doors is outside the scope of the social contract. Such rules, therefore, have no claim on us.

2. *Why is it rational for us to follow the moral rules?* We *agree* to follow the moral rules because we benefit from living in a place where the rules are accepted. However, we *actually do* follow the rules—we keep our end of the bargain—because the rules will be enforced, and it is rational for us to avoid punishment. Why don't you kidnap your boss? Because you might get caught.

But what if you think you won't get caught? Why follow the rules then? To answer this question, first note that you don't want *other* people to break the rules when they think they can avoid punishment—you don't want other people to commit murder, assault, and so on, just because they think they can get away with it. After all, they might be murdering or assaulting *you*. For this reason, we want others to accept the contract in more than a frivolous or lighthearted way. We want them to form a *firm intention* to hold up their end of the bargain; we want them to become the sort of people who won't be tempted to stray. And, of course, they will demand the same of us, as part of the agreement. But once we have this firm intention, it is rational to act on it. Why don't you kidnap your boss, when you think you can get away with it? Because you've made a firm decision not to be that sort of person.

3. *Under what circumstances is it rational to break the rules?* We agree to obey the rules on the condition that others obey them as well. But when someone else breaks the rules, he releases us from our obligations toward him. For example, suppose someone refuses to help you in circumstances in which he clearly should. If later on he needs your help, you may rightly feel that you have no duty to help him.

The same point explains why punishing criminals is acceptable. Lawbreakers are treated differently from other citizens—in punishing them, we treat them in ways that are normally forbidden. Why can we do this? Remember that the rules apply to you only if other people also follow them. So, you may disregard those rules when dealing with someone who doesn't follow them. In breaking the rules, the criminal thus leaves himself open to retaliation. This explains why it is legitimate for the government to enforce the law.

4. *How much can morality demand of us?* Morality seems to require that we be impartial, that is, that we give no greater weight to our own interests than to the interests of others. But suppose you face a situation in which you must choose between your own death and the deaths of five other people. Impartiality, it seems, would require you to choose your own death; after all, there are five of them and only one of you. Are you morally bound to sacrifice yourself?

Philosophers have often felt uneasy about this sort of example; they have felt instinctively that somehow there are limits to what morality can demand of us. Therefore, they have traditionally said that such heroic actions are *supererogatory*— that is, above and beyond the call of duty, admirable when they occur but not morally required. Yet it is hard to explain why such actions are not required. If morality demands impartial behavior, and it is better that one person die rather than five, then you should be required to sacrifice yourself.

What does the Social Contract Theory say about this? Suppose the question is whether to have the rule "If you can save many lives by sacrificing your own life, then you must do so." Would it be rational to accept this rule, on the condition that everyone else accepts it? Presumably, it would be. After all, each of us is more likely to benefit from this rule than to be harmed by it—you're more likely to be among those saved than to be the one and only person who gives up her life. Thus, it may seem that the Social Contract Theory does require moral heroism.

But this is not so. On the Social Contract Theory, morality consists in the rules that rational people will accept *on the condition that others accept them as well.* However, it would not be rational to make an agreement that we don't expect others to follow. Can we expect other people to follow this rule of self-sacrifice—can we expect strangers to give up their lives for us? We cannot. Most people won't be that benevolent, even if they have promised to be. Can we expect the threat of punishment to *make them* that benevolent? Again, we cannot; people's fear of death is likely to overwhelm any fear they have of punishment. Thus, there is a natural limit to the amount of self-sacrifice that the social contract can require: Rational people will not agree to rules so demanding that others won't follow them. In this way, the Social Contract Theory explains a feature of morality that other theories may remain silent on.

6.4. The Problem of Civil Disobedience

Moral theories should help us understand concrete moral issues. The Social Contract Theory in particular should help us understand issues about social institutions—after all, explaining the proper function of those institutions is one of the main goals of the theory. So let's consider again our obligation to obey the law. Are we ever justified in breaking the law? If so, when?

The great modern examples of civil disobedience are taken from the Indian independence movement led by Mohandas K. Gandhi (1869–1948) and the American civil rights movement led by Martin Luther King Jr. (1929–1968). Both movements were characterized by public, conscientious, non-violent refusal to comply with the law. In 1930, Gandhi and his followers marched to the coastal village of Dandi, where they defied British law by distilling salt from saltwater. The British had been controlling salt production so they could force the Indian peasants to buy it at high prices. In America, Dr. King led the Montgomery Bus Boycott, which began after Rosa Parks was arrested on December 1, 1955, for refusing to give up her bus seat to a white man. Parks was defying one of the "Jim Crow" laws designed to enforce racial segregation in the South.

Gandhi and King, the two greatest proponents of nonviolence in the 20th century, were both murdered by gunfire.

Their movements had importantly different goals. Gandhi and his followers did not recognize the right of the British to govern India; they wanted to replace British rule with an entirely different system. King and his followers, however, did not question the legitimacy of the American government. Rather, they objected only to particular laws and social policies that they felt were unjust—so unjust, in fact, that they refused to comply with them.

In his "Letter from the Birmingham City Jail" (1963), King describes the frustration and anger that arise

> when you have seen vicious mobs lynch your mothers and fathers at will and drown your sisters and brothers at whim; when you have seen hate-filled policemen curse, kick, brutalize and even kill your black brothers and sisters with impunity; when you see the vast majority of your twenty million Negro brothers smothering in an airtight cage of poverty in the midst of an affluent society; when you suddenly find your tongue twisted and your speech stammering as you seek to explain to your six-year-old daughter why she can't go to the public amusement park that has just been advertised on television, and see tears welling up in her little eyes when she is told that Funtown is closed to colored children, and see the depressing clouds of inferiority begin to form in her little mental sky.

The problem was not only that racial segregation, with all its attendant evils, was enforced by social custom; it was a matter of *law* as well, law that black citizens were denied a voice in formulating. When urged to rely on ordinary democratic processes, King pointed out that all attempts to use these processes had failed. And as for "democracy," he said, that word had no meaning to southern blacks: "Throughout the state of Alabama all types of conniving methods are used to prevent Negroes from becoming registered voters and there are some counties without a single Negro registered to vote despite the fact that the Negro constitutes a majority of the population." King believed, therefore, that blacks had no choice but to defy the unjust laws and to accept the consequences by going to jail.

Today we remember King as a great moral leader. At the time, however, his strategy of civil disobedience was highly controversial. Many liberals expressed sympathy for his goals but didn't agree with his tactic of breaking the law. An article in the *New York State Bar Journal* in 1965 expressed the typical worries. After assuring his readers that "long before Dr. King was born, I espoused, and still espouse, the cause of civil rights for all people," Louis Waldman, a prominent New York lawyer, argues:

> Those who assert rights under the Constitution and the laws made thereunder must abide by that Constitution and the law, if that Constitution is to survive. They cannot pick and choose; they cannot say they will abide by those laws which they think are just and refuse to abide by those laws which they think are unjust. . . .
>
> The country, therefore, cannot accept Dr. King's doctrine that he and his followers will pick and choose, knowing that it is illegal to do so. I say, such doctrine is not only illegal and for that reason alone should be abandoned, but that it is also immoral, destructive of the principles of democratic government, and a danger to the very civil rights Dr. King seeks to promote.

Waldman had a point: If our legal system is basically decent, then defying the law is on its face a bad thing, because open defiance of particular laws might weaken people's respect for the law generally. To meet this objection, King sometimes said that the evils he opposed were so serious, so numerous, and so difficult to fight that civil disobedience was justified as a last resort. The end justifies the means, though the means are regrettable. This argument may be enough to answer Waldman's objections. But there is a more profound reply available.

According to the Social Contract Theory, we are obligated to obey the law because we each participate in a social system that promises more benefits than burdens. The benefits are the benefits of social living: We escape the state of nature and live in a society in which we are secure and enjoy basic rights. To gain these benefits, we agree to uphold the institutions that make them possible. This means that we must obey the law, pay our taxes, and so forth—these are the burdens we accept in return.

But what if some citizens are denied their basic rights? What if the police, instead of protecting them, "curse, kick, brutalize and even kill [them] with impunity"? What if some groups of people are denied a decent education while they and their families are "smothering in an airtight cage of poverty"? Under such circumstances, the social contract is not being honored. By asking the disadvantaged group to obey the law and respect society's institutions, we are asking them to accept the burdens of social living while being denied its benefits.

This line of reasoning suggests that civil disobedience is not an undesirable "last resort" for socially disenfranchised groups. Rather, it is the most natural and reasonable means of expressing protest. For when the disadvantaged are denied the benefits of social living, they are released from the contract that would otherwise require them to follow society's rules. This is the deepest argument for civil disobedience, and the Social Contract Theory presents it clearly and forcefully.

6.5. Difficulties for the Theory

The Social Contract Theory is one of the major options in contemporary moral philosophy, along with Utilitarianism, Kantianism, and Virtue Ethics. It is easy to see why; the theory seems to explain a great deal about moral life. Two important objections, however, have been made against it.

First, it is said that the Social Contract Theory is based on a historical fiction. We are asked to imagine that people once lived in isolation from one another, that they found this intolerable, and that they eventually banded together, agreeing to follow social rules of mutual benefit. But none of this ever happened. It is just a fantasy. So of what relevance is it? To be sure, if people *had* come together in this way, we could explain their obligations to one another as the theory suggests: They would be obligated to obey the rules that they had agreed to obey. But even then, there would be problems. Was the agreement unanimous? If not, what about the people who didn't sign up—are they *not* required to act morally? And if the contract was made a long time ago by our ancestors, why should we be bound to it? But anyway, there never was such a contract, and so nothing can be explained by appealing to it. As one critic wisecracked, the social contract "isn't worth the paper it's not written on."

To be sure, none of us ever signed a "real" contract—there is no piece of paper bearing our signatures. Immigrants, who promise to obey the law when they are granted citizenship, are the exception. The contract theorist might say, however, that a social arrangement like the one described does exist, for all of us: There is a set of rules that everyone recognizes as binding on them, and we all benefit from the fact that these rules are generally followed. Each of us accepts the benefits conferred by this arrangement; and, more than that, we expect and encourage other people to observe the rules. This is a description of the actual world; it is not fictitious. And, by accepting the benefits of this arrangement, we incur an obligation to do our part— which at least means that we should follow the rules. We are thus bound by an *implicit* social contract. It is "implicit" because we become a party to it not by explicitly making a promise, but by accepting the benefits of social living.

Thus, the story of the "social contract" need not be intended as a description of historical events. Rather, it is a useful analytical tool, based on the idea that we may understand our moral obligations *as if* they had arisen in this way. Consider the following situation: Suppose you come upon a group of people playing an elaborate game. It looks like fun, and you join in. After a while, however, you begin to break some of the rules, because that looks like more fun. When the other players protest, you say that you never promised to follow the rules. However, your remark is irrelevant. Perhaps nobody promised to obey; but, by joining the game, each person implicitly agreed to abide by the rules that make the game possible. It is *as though* they had all agreed. Morality is like this. The "game" is social living; the rules, which make the game possible, are the rules of morality.

That response to the first objection, however, is ineffective. When a game is in progress, and you join in, it is obvious that you *choose* to join in, because you could have just walked away. For that reason, you must respect the game's rules, or you will rightly be regarded as a nuisance. By contrast, somebody born into today's big cooperative world does not choose to join it; nobody chooses to be born. And then, once a person has grown up, the costs of leaving that world are severe. How could you opt out? You might become a survivalist and never use electricity, roads, the water service, and so on. But that would be a great burden. Alternatively, you might leave the country. But what if you don't like the social rules that exist in any of the other countries, either? Moreover, as David Hume

(1711–1776) observed, many people are not "free to leave their country" in any meaningful sense:

> Can we seriously say that a poor peasant . . . has a free choice to leave his country, when he knows no foreign language or manners, and lives from day to day by the small wages which he acquires? We may as well assert that a man, by remaining [on a ship], freely consents to the dominion of the master, though he was carried on board while asleep, and must leap into the ocean and perish the moment he leaves.

Thus, life is not like joining a game, whose rules you may reject by walking away. Rather, life is like being thrust into a game you can't walk away from. The contract theorist has not explained why one must obey the rules of such a game.

Does the first objection therefore refute the Social Contract Theory? I don't think so. The contract theorist may say this: Participating in a sensible social scheme is rational; it really is in one's best interest. *This is why the rules are valid*—because they benefit those who live under them. If someone doesn't agree to the rules, the rules still apply to him; he's just being irrational. Suppose, for example, that a survivalist forgoes the benefits of social living. May he then refuse to pay his taxes? He may not, because even he would be better off paying his taxes *and* enjoying the benefits of clean water, paved roads, indoor plumbing, and so on. The survivalist might not want to play the game, but the rules still apply to him, because it would really and truly be in his interest to join in.

This defense of the Social Contract Theory abandons the idea that morality is based on an agreement. However, it holds fast to the idea that morality consists in rules of mutual benefit. It also accords with the definition of the theory we gave earlier: *Morality consists in the set of rules, governing behavior, that rational people will accept, on the condition that others accept them as well.* Rational people will agree to the mutually beneficial rules.

The second objection is more troubling. Some individuals cannot benefit us. Thus, according to the Social Contract Theory, these individuals have no claim on us, and we may ignore their interests when we're writing up the rules of society. The moral rules will therefore let us treat these individuals in any way whatsoever. This implication of the theory is unacceptable.

There would be at least four vulnerable groups:

- Human infants
- Nonhuman animals
- Future generations
- Oppressed populations

Suppose, for example, that a sadist wanted to torment a cat or a small child. *He* would not benefit from a system of rules forbidding the torture of infants and animals; after all, the infant and the cat cannot benefit him, and he wants to practice his cruel behavior. Of course, the infant's parents, and the cat's owners, would be indirectly harmed under such a system, and they might want to retaliate against the sadist. In such a situation, it is hard to know what moral rules would be valid. But suppose the sadist found some abandoned children or some stray cats out in the woods. Now the Social Contract Theory cannot condemn him even if he commits acts of the greatest cruelty.

Or consider future generations. They cannot benefit us; we'll be dead before they are even born. But we can profit at their expense. Why shouldn't we run up the national debt? Why shouldn't we pollute the lakes and coat the skies with carbon dioxide? Why shouldn't we bury toxic waste in containers that will fall apart in a hundred years? It would not be against *our* interests to allow such actions; it would only harm our descendants. So, we may do so. Or consider oppressed populations. When the Europeans colonized new lands, why weren't they morally allowed to enslave the native inhabitants? After all, the native inhabitants did not have the weapons to put up a good fight. The Europeans could benefit most by creating a society in which the native inhabitants would be their slaves.

This objection does not concern some minor aspect of the theory; it goes right to the root of the tree. The Social Contract Theory is grounded in self-interest and reciprocity; thus, it seems unable to recognize the moral duties we have to individuals who cannot benefit us.

CHAPTER 7

The Utilitarian Approach

The greatest happiness of the greatest number is the foundation of
morals and legislation.

JEREMY BENTHAM, *COLLECTED WORKS* (1843)

7.1. The Revolution in Ethics

The late 18th and 19th centuries witnessed an astonishing
series of upheavals: The modern nation-state emerged from
the French Revolution and the wreckage of the Napoleonic
empire; the revolutions of 1848 showed the transforming
power of the ideas of "liberty, equality, and fraternity"; in the
New World, America was born, sporting a new kind of constitution; and the American Civil War (1861–1865) would finish
off slavery in Western civilization. All the while, the Indus-
trial Revolution was bringing about a complete restructuring
of society.

It is not surprising that new ideas about ethics emerged
during this era. In particular, Jeremy Bentham (1748–1832)
made a powerful argument for a novel conception of morality.
Morality, he urged, is not about pleasing God, nor is it about
being faithful to abstract rules. Rather, morality is about making the world as happy as possible. Bentham believed in one
ultimate moral principle, namely, the Principle of Utility. This
principle requires us, in all circumstances, to produce the most
happiness that we can.

Bentham was the leader of a group of philosophical
radicals whose aim was to reform the laws and institutions of
England along utilitarian lines. One of his followers was James
Mill, the distinguished Scottish philosopher, historian, and
economist. James Mill's son, John Stuart Mill (1806–1873),
would become the leading advocate of utilitarian moral theory.

John Stuart's advocacy was even more elegant and persuasive than Bentham's. Mill's short book *Utilitarianism* (1861) is still required reading for serious students of ethics.

At first glance, the Principle of Utility may not seem like such a radical idea; in fact, it may seem too obvious to mention. Who *doesn't* believe that we should oppose suffering and promote happiness? Yet, in their own way, Bentham and Mill were as revolutionary as the other two great intellectual innovators of the 19th century, Darwin and Marx.

To understand why the Principle of Utility was so radical, consider what it *leaves out* of morality: Gone are all references to God or to abstract moral rules "written in the heavens." Morality is no longer conceived of as faithfulness to some divinely given code or some set of inflexible rules. As Peter Singer (1946–) would later put it, morality is not "a system of nasty puritanical prohibitions . . . designed to stop people [from] having fun." Rather, the point of morality is the happiness of beings in this world, and nothing more; and we are permitted—even required—to do whatever is necessary to promote that happiness. This was a revolutionary idea.

As I said, the utilitarians were social reformers as well as philosophers. They intended their doctrine to make a difference, not only in thought but in practice. To illustrate this, we will briefly examine the implications of their ideas for three practical issues: euthanasia, marijuana, and the treatment of nonhuman animals. These issues do not exhaust the practical applications of Utilitarianism; nor are they necessarily the ones that utilitarians would find most pressing. But they do give us a good sense of how utilitarians approach moral issues.

7.2. First Example: Euthanasia

Sigmund Freud (1856–1939), the legendary psychologist, was diagnosed with oral cancer after a lifetime of cigar smoking. During his final years, Freud's health went up and down, but in early 1939 a large swelling formed in the back of his mouth, and he would have no more good days. Freud's cancer was active and inoperable, and he was also suffering from heart failure. As his bones decayed, they cast off a foul smell, driving away his favorite dog. Mosquito netting had to be draped over his bed to keep flies away.

On September 21, at the age of 83, Freud took his friend and personal physician, Max Schur, by the hand and said, "My dear Schur, you certainly remember our first talk. You promised me then not to forsake me when my time comes. Now it's nothing but torture and makes no sense any more." Forty years earlier Freud had written, "What has the individual come to . . . if one no longer dares to disclose that it is this or that man's turn to die?" Dr. Schur said he understood Freud's request. He injected Freud with a drug in order to end his life. "He soon felt relief," Dr. Schur wrote, "and fell into a peaceful sleep."

Did Max Schur do anything wrong? On the one hand, he was motivated by noble sentiments—he loved his friend and wanted to relieve his misery. Moreover, Freud had asked to die. All this argues for a lenient judgment. On the other hand, what Schur did was morally wrong, according to the dominant moral tradition in our culture.

That tradition is Christianity. Christianity holds that human life is a gift from God, and only God may decide to end it. The early church prohibited all killing, believing that Jesus's teachings permitted no exceptions to the rule. Later, the church recognized some exceptions, such as capital punishment and killing in war. But suicide and euthanasia remained forbidden. To summarize the church's doctrine, theologians formulated the rule: *the intentional killing of innocent people is always wrong.* This idea, more than any other, has shaped Western attitudes about the morality of killing. Thus we may be reluctant to excuse Max Schur, even though he acted from noble motives. He intentionally killed an innocent person; therefore, according to our tradition, what he did was wrong.

Utilitarianism takes a very different approach. It asks: which action available to Max Schur would have produced the greatest balance of happiness over unhappiness? The person whose happiness was most at stake was Sigmund Freud. If Schur had not killed him, Freud would have lived on, in wretched pain. How much unhappiness would this have involved? It is hard to say precisely; but Freud's condition was so bad that he preferred death. Killing him ended his agony. Therefore, utilitarians have concluded that euthanasia, in such a case, is morally right.

Although this argument is very different from arguments in the Christian tradition, the classical utilitarians did not think they were advocating an atheistic or antireligious philosophy.

Bentham thought that the faithful would endorse the utilitarian standpoint if only they viewed God as *benevolent*. He writes:

> The dictates of religion would coincide, in all cases, with those of utility, were the Being, who is the object of religion, universally supposed to be as benevolent as he is supposed to be wise and powerful. . . . But among the [advocates] of religion . . . there seem to be but few . . . who are real believers in his benevolence. They call him benevolent in words, but they do not mean that he is so in reality.

The morality of mercy killing might be a case in point. How, Bentham might ask, could a benevolent God forbid the killing of Sigmund Freud? If someone were to say, "God is caring and loving—but He forbids us from putting Freud out of his misery," this would be exactly what Bentham means by "calling him benevolent in words, but not meaning that he is so in reality."

The majority of religious people disagree with Bentham, and not only our moral tradition but our legal tradition has evolved under the influence of Christianity. Among Western nations, euthanasia is legal in only a handful of countries. In the United States, it is simply murder, and a doctor who intentionally kills her patient could spend the rest of her life in prison. What would Utilitarianism say about this? If euthanasia is moral, on the utilitarian view, should it also be legal?

In general, we don't want to outlaw morally acceptable behavior. Bentham was trained in the law, and he thought of the Principle of Utility as a guide for both legislators and ordinary people. The purpose of the law, he thought, is to promote the welfare of all citizens. In order to serve this purpose, the law should restrict people's freedom as little as possible. In particular, no activity should be outlawed unless that activity is harmful or dangerous to others. Bentham opposed, for example, laws regulating the sexual conduct of consenting adults. But it was Mill who gave this principle its most eloquent expression, in his book *On Liberty* (1859):

> The only purpose for which power can be rightfully exercised over any member of a civilized community, against his will, is to prevent harm to others. His own good, either physical or moral, is not a sufficient warrant. . . . Over himself, over his own body and mind, the individual is sovereign.

Thus, for the classical utilitarians, laws against euthanasia are unjustified restrictions on people's ability to control their own lives. When Max Schur killed Sigmund Freud, he was helping Freud end his life in the manner that Freud had chosen. No harm was caused to anyone else, and so it was no one else's business. Bentham himself is said to have requested euthanasia in his final days. However, we do not know whether his request was granted.

7.3. Second Example: Marijuana

William Bennett was America's first "drug czar." From 1989 to 1991, as President George H. W. Bush's top advisor on drug policy, he advocated the aggressive enforcement of U.S. drug laws. Bennett, who holds a Ph.D. in philosophy, said, "The simple fact is that drug use is wrong. And the moral argument, in the end, is the most compelling argument." Bennett's "moral argument," it seems, is just the assertion that drug use is wrong, by its very nature. What would utilitarians think about this? For them, there is no "simple fact" as to whether drug use is immoral. Rather, the moral argument must address the complex question of whether drug use increases or decreases happiness. Let's think about one drug in particular: marijuana. What would a utilitarian say about the ethics of pot?

People have strong feelings on this topic. Younger people who use drugs might be defensive and deny that pot causes any harm at all; older people who don't use drugs might be judgmental while failing to distinguish marijuana from harder drugs like cocaine and methamphetamine. A good utilitarian will ignore such feelings. What are the pros and cons of marijuana, according to Utilitarianism?

The main benefit of pot is the pleasure it brings. Not only is marijuana enormously relaxing, but marijuana can greatly enhance the pleasure of sensory activities, such as eating, listening to music, and having sex. This fact is almost never mentioned in public discussion; people seem to assume that enjoyment is irrelevant to morality. Utilitarians, however, disagree. For them, the whole issue is whether pot increases or decreases happiness. And utilitarians do not believe in "bad pleasures." If something feels good, then it is good, at least to that extent.

How pleasurable is marijuana? Some people love it; some people don't like it; and a lot depends on whether it is used in a comfortable setting. Thus, it is hard to generalize. But the facts suggest that many people enjoy getting high. Marijuana is the most popular illicit drug in America: One-third of Americans have tried it; 6% have used it in the past month; and Americans spend more than $10 billion per year on it, despite the threat of prison.

What unhappiness does marijuana cause? Some of the charges made against it are unfounded. First, marijuana does not cause violence; pot tends to make people passive, not aggressive. Second, marijuana is not a "gateway drug" that causes people to crave and use harder drugs. Often, people do use pot before using harder drugs, but that is because pot is so widely available. In neighborhoods where crack cocaine is easier to get, people usually try crack first. Third, marijuana is not highly addictive. According to the experts, it is less addictive than caffeine. Utilitarians do not want to base their assessment on false information.

Marijuana, however, does have some real disadvantages, which the utilitarian must weigh against the benefits. First, some people do get addicted to pot. Although marijuana withdrawal is not as traumatic as, say, heroin withdrawal, quitting is unpleasant for the addict. Second, long-term heavy use can cause mild cognitive damage, which may decrease happiness. Third, getting high all the time would make a person unproductive. Fourth, *smoking* pot is bad for your respiratory system; one joint may be as bad for your lungs as about six cigarettes. However, ingesting marijuana in other ways—for example, by baking it into brownies—should not be bad for your lungs at all.

What do utilitarians conclude from all this? When we look at the harms and benefits, the occasional use of pot hardly seems to be a moral issue at all; there are no known disadvantages to it. Thus, utilitarians consider casual use to be a matter of personal preference. Heavy marijuana use raises more complex issues. Does the pleasure one gets from long-term, heavy use outweigh the disadvantages? It probably depends on the person. Anyway, the question is so difficult that utilitarians may disagree on the answer.

So far we've been discussing the individual's decision of whether to use marijuana. What about the law—should pot be illegal, according to Utilitarianism? The fact that many people enjoy getting high is a strong reason to legalize the drug, according to Utilitarianism. What other factors are relevant?

If marijuana were legal, more people would use it, and several worries arise from that fact: society as a whole might become less productive; taxpayers might get stuck with the medical bills of heavy users; and more people might drive while high. It should be noted, however, that marijuana impairs driving ability only slightly, because people who are stoned drive cautiously and defensively.

On the other hand, society would be better off insofar as marijuana replaced alcohol as a drug of abuse: stoned citizens are unproductive, but alcoholics miss even more work because of the bad morning-after hangover; alcoholism is especially expensive in terms of health care; alcohol impairs driving ability much more than pot does; and, finally, drunks are far more violent than potheads. Thus, one benefit of legalizing pot would be fewer alcoholics, even if there would be more potheads.

Also, there are two big costs to maintaining the current laws. The first is the lost revenue for society. With marijuana illegal, society spends money on criminal enforcement; with marijuana legal, society collects money from taxing pot. Legalizing marijuana in the United States would save about $7.7 billion per year in enforcement costs, and it would generate between $2.4 and $6.2 billion in tax revenue, depending on whether pot was taxed normally or at the higher rate at which alcohol and tobacco are now taxed.

But the greatest cost is the harm done to the offenders. In the United States, over 700,000 people are arrested each year for possession of marijuana, and more than 44,000 people are currently in prison for marijuana offenses. Not only is being arrested and incarcerated horrible, but ex-cons have trouble finding decent jobs. Utilitarians care about these harms, even though the harms are inflicted on lawbreakers who knew they might be punished.

Thus, almost all utilitarians favor the legalization of marijuana. On the whole, marijuana is less harmful than alcohol or cigarettes, which Western societies already tolerate. However, utilitarians must be flexible; if new evidence emerges, showing marijuana to be more harmful than was previously thought, then the utilitarian view might change.

7.4. Third Example: Nonhuman Animals

The treatment of animals has traditionally been regarded as a trivial matter. Christians believe that man alone is made in God's image and that animals do not have souls. Thus, by the natural order of things, we can treat animals in any way we like. Saint Thomas Aquinas (1225–1274) summed up the traditional view when he wrote:

> Hereby is refuted the error of those who said it is sinful for a man to kill brute animals; for by the divine providence they are intended for man's use in the natural order. Hence it is not wrong for man to make use of them, either by killing them or in any other way whatever.

But isn't it wrong to be *cruel* to animals? Aquinas concedes that it is, but he says the reason has to do with human welfare, not the welfare of the animals:

> And if any passages of Holy Scripture seem to forbid us to be cruel to brute animals, for instance to kill a bird with its young, this is either to remove man's thoughts from being cruel to other men, lest through being cruel to animals one becomes cruel to human beings; or because injury to an animal leads to the temporal hurt of man, either of the doer of the deed, or of another.

Thus, people and animals are in separate moral categories. Animals have no moral standing of their own; we are free to treat them in any way we please.

Put so bluntly, the traditional doctrine might make us a little nervous: It seems extreme in its lack of concern for nonhuman animals, many of which are, after all, intelligent and sensitive creatures. Yet only a little reflection is needed to see how much of our conduct is actually guided by this doctrine. We eat animals; we use them as experimental subjects in our laboratories; we use their skins for clothing and their heads as wall ornaments; we make them the objects of our amusement in circuses and rodeos; and we track them down and kill them for sport.

If one is uncomfortable with the theological "justification" of these practices, Western philosophers have offered plenty of secular ones. Philosophers have said that animals are not *rational*, that they lack the ability to *speak*, or that they are simply not *human*—and all these are given as reasons why their interests lie outside the sphere of moral concern.

The utilitarians, however, would have none of this. On their view, what matters is not whether an animal has a soul, is rational, or any of the rest. All that matters is whether it can experience happiness and unhappiness. If an animal can suffer, then we have a duty to take that into account when deciding what to do. In fact, Bentham argues that whether an animal is human or nonhuman is just as irrelevant as whether the animal is black or white. He writes:

> The day *may* come when the rest of the animal creation may acquire those rights which never could have been withholden from them but by the hand of tyranny. The French have already discovered that the blackness of the skin is no reason why a human being should be abandoned without redress to the caprice of a tormentor. It may one day come to be recognized that the number of the legs, the villosity of the skin, or the termination of the *os sacrum* are reasons equally insufficient for abandoning a sensitive being to the same fate. What else is it that should trace the insuperable line? Is it the faculty of reason, or perhaps the faculty of discourse? But a full-grown horse or dog is beyond comparison a more rational, as well as a more conversable animal, than an infant of a day or a week or even a month old. But suppose they were otherwise, what would it avail? The question is not, Can they *reason?* nor Can they *talk?* but, Can they *suffer?*

If a human is tormented, why is it wrong? Because that person suffers. Similarly, if a nonhuman is tormented, it also suffers. Whether it is a *human* or an *animal* that suffers is simply irrelevant. To Bentham and Mill, this line of reasoning was conclusive. Humans and nonhumans are equally entitled to moral concern.

This view may seem as extreme, in the opposite direction, as the traditional view that grants animals no moral standing at all. Are animals really to be regarded as the equals of humans? In some sense, Bentham and Mill thought so, but they did not believe that animals and humans must always be treated in the same way. There are factual differences between them that will often justify differences in treatment. For example, because of their intellectual capacities, humans can take pleasure in things that nonhumans cannot enjoy—mathematics, literature, strategy games, and so on. And, similarly, humans' superior capacities make them capable of frustrations and disappointments that other animals cannot experience. Thus, our duty to promote happiness entails a duty to promote those special enjoyments for humans, as well as to prevent any special harms they might suffer. At the same time, however, we have a moral duty to take into account the suffering of animals, and their suffering counts equally with any similar suffering experienced by a human.

In 1970 the British psychologist Richard D. Ryder coined the term "speciesism" to refer to the idea that animal interests matter less than human interests. Utilitarians believe that speciesism is discrimination against other species, just as racism is discrimination against other races. Ryder wonders how we can possibly justify allowing experiments such as these:

- In Maryland in 1996, scientists used beagle dogs to study septic shock. They cut holes in the dogs' throats and placed *E. coli*-infected clots into their stomachs. Within three weeks, most of the dogs had died.
- In Taiwan in 1997, scientists dropped weights onto rats' spines in order to study spinal injury. The researchers found that greater injuries were caused by dropping the weights from greater heights.
- Since the 1990s, chimpanzees, monkeys, dogs, cats, and rodents have been used to study alcoholism. After addicting the animals to alcohol, scientists have observed such symptoms as vomiting, tremor, anxiety, and seizures. When the animals are in alcoholic withdrawal, scientists have induced convulsions by lifting them by their tails, by giving them electric shocks, and by injecting chemicals into their brains.

The utilitarian argument is simple enough. We should judge actions right or wrong depending on whether they cause more happiness or unhappiness. The animals in these experiments were obviously caused terrible suffering. Was there any compensating gain in happiness that justified it? Was greater unhappiness being prevented, for other animals or for humans? If not, the experiments were morally unacceptable.

This style of argument does not imply that all animal experiments are immoral. Rather, it suggests judging each one on its own merits. The utilitarian principle does, however, imply that experiments that cause a lot of pain require significant justification. We cannot simply assume that, in dealing with nonhumans, anything goes.

But criticizing animal experiments is too easy for most of us. We may feel self-righteous or superior because we do not do such research ourselves. All of us, however, are involved in cruelty when we eat meat. The facts about meat production are more disturbing than any facts about animal experimentation.

Most people believe, in a vague way, that slaughterhouses are unpleasant, but that animals raised for food are otherwise treated humanely. In fact, farm animals live in abhorrent conditions before being taken off to slaughter. Veal calves, for example, spend 24 hours per day in pens so small that they cannot turn around, lie down comfortably, or even twist their heads around to get rid of parasites. The producers put them in tiny pens to save money and to keep their meat tender. The cows clearly miss their mothers, and like human infants, they want something to suck, so they try in vain to suck the sides of their wooden stalls. The calves are also fed a diet deficient in iron and roughage, in order to keep their meat pale and tasty. Their craving for iron becomes so strong that they will lick at their own urine, if they're allowed to turn around—which normally they would never do. Without roughage, the calves cannot form a cud to chew. For this reason, they cannot be given straw bedding, because they would eat it, in an attempt to consume roughage. So, for these animals, the slaughterhouse is not an unpleasant end to an otherwise contented existence.

The veal calf is just one example. Chickens, turkeys, pigs, and adult cows all live in horrible conditions before being slaughtered. The utilitarian argument on these matters is simple enough. The system of meat production causes enormous suffering for the animals with no compensating benefits. Therefore, we should abandon that system. We should either become vegetarians or else treat our animals humanely before killing them.

What is most revolutionary in all this is simply the idea that the interests of nonhuman animals *count*. We normally assume that human beings alone are worthy of moral consideration.

Utilitarianism challenges that assumption and insists that the moral community must be expanded to include all creatures whose interests can be affected by what we do. Human beings are in many ways special, and an adequate morality must acknowledge that. But we are not the only animals on this planet, and an adequate morality must acknowledge that fact as well.

CHAPTER 8

The Debate over Utilitarianism

The creed which accepts . . . the Greatest Happiness
Principle . . . holds that actions are right . . . as they tend to promote
happiness, wrong as they tend to produce the reverse of happiness.
JOHN STUART MILL, *UTILITARIANISM* (1861)

Man does not strive after happiness; only the Englishman does that.
FRIEDRICH NIETZSCHE, *TWILIGHT OF THE IDOLS* (1889)

8.1. The Classical Version of the Theory

Classical Utilitarianism can be summed up in three propositions: (a) The morality of an action depends solely on the consequences of the action; nothing else matters. (b) An action's
consequences matter only insofar as they involve the greater
or lesser happiness of individuals. (c) In the assessment of
consequences, each individual's happiness gets "equal consideration." This means that equal amounts of happiness always
count equally; nobody's well-being matters more just because
he is rich, let's say, or powerful, or handsome. Morally, everyone counts the same. According to Classical Utilitarianism, an
action is right if it produces the greatest overall balance of happiness over unhappiness.

Classical Utilitarianism was developed and defended by
three of the greatest philosophers in 19th-century England:
Jeremy Bentham (1748–1832), John Stuart Mill (1806–1873),
and Henry Sidgwick (1838–1900). Thanks in part to their work,
Utilitarianism has had a profound influence on modern thinking. Most moral philosophers, however, reject the theory. In what
follows, we will discuss some of the objections that have made the
theory unpopular. In examining these arguments, we will also be
pondering some of the deepest questions in ethical theory.

110

8.2. Is Pleasure All That Matters?

The question *What things are good?* is different from the question *What actions are right?* and Utilitarianism answers the second question by reference to the first. Right actions are the ones that produce the most good. But what is good? The utilitarian reply is: happiness. As Mill puts it, "The utilitarian doctrine is that happiness is desirable, and the only thing desirable, as an end; all other things being only desirable as means to that end."

But what is happiness? According to the classical utilitarians, happiness is pleasure. Utilitarians understand "pleasure" broadly, to include all mental states that feel good. A sense of accomplishment, a delicious taste, and the heightened awareness that comes at the climax of a suspenseful movie are all examples of pleasure. The thesis that pleasure is the one ultimate good—and pain the one ultimate evil—has been known since antiquity as Hedonism. The idea that things are good or bad because of how they make us *feel* has always had a following in philosophy. Yet a little reflection seems to reveal flaws in this theory.

Consider these two examples:

- *You think someone is your friend, but he ridicules you behind your back.* No one tells you, so you never know. Is this unfortunate for you? Hedonists would have to say it is not, because you are never caused any pain. Yet we believe that there is something bad going on. You are being mistreated, even though you are unaware of it and suffer no unhappiness.

- *A promising young pianist's hands are injured in a car accident so that she can no longer play.* Why is this bad for her? Hedonists would say it is bad because it causes her pain and eliminates a source of joy for her. But suppose she finds something else that she enjoys just as much—suppose, for example, she gets as much pleasure from watching hockey on TV as she once got from playing the piano. Why is her accident now a tragedy? The hedonist can only say that she will feel frustrated and upset whenever she thinks of what might have been, and *that* is her misfortune. But this explanation gets things backward. It is not as though, by feeling upset, she has turned a neutral situation into a bad one. On the contrary, the bad situation is what made her unhappy. She might have become a great pianist, and now she will not. We cannot eliminate the tragedy by getting her to cheer up and watch hockey.

Both of these examples rely on the same idea: We value things other than pleasure. For example, we value artistic creativity and friendship. These things make us happy, but that's not the only reason we value them. It seems like a misfortune to lose them, even if there is no loss of happiness.

For this reason, most present-day utilitarians reject the classical assumption of Hedonism. Some of them bypass the question of what's good, saying only that right actions are the ones that have the best results, however that is measured. Other utilitarians, such as the English philosopher G. E. Moore (1873–1958), have compiled short lists of things to be regarded as valuable in themselves. Moore suggested that there are three obvious intrinsic goods—pleasure, friendship, and aesthetic enjoyment—and so right actions are those actions that increase the world's supply of these things. Still others say that we should act so as to maximize the satisfaction of people's *preferences*. We won't discuss the merits and demerits of these theories of the good. I mention them only to note that, although Hedonism has largely been rejected, contemporary utilitarians have not found it difficult to carry on.

8.3. Are Consequences All That Matter?

To determine whether an action is right, utilitarians believe that we should look at *what will happen as a result of doing it*. This idea is central to the theory. If things other than consequences are important in determining what is right, then Utilitarianism is incorrect. Here are three arguments that attack the theory at just this point.

Justice. In 1965, writing in the racially charged climate of the American civil rights movement, H. J. McCloskey asks us to consider the following case:

> Suppose a utilitarian were visiting an area in which there was racial strife, and that, during his visit, a Negro rapes a white woman, and that race riots occur as a result of

the crime. . . . Suppose too that our utilitarian is in the area of the crime when it is committed such that his testimony would bring about the conviction of [whomever he accuses]. If he knows that a quick arrest will stop the riots and lynchings, surely, as a utilitarian, he must conclude that he has a duty to bear false witness in order to bring about the punishment of an innocent person.

Such an accusation would have bad consequences—the innocent man would be convicted—but there would be enough good consequences to outweigh them: The riots and lynchings would be stopped, and many lives would be saved. The best outcome would thus be achieved by bearing false witness; therefore, according to Utilitarianism, lying is the thing to do. But, the argument continues, it would be wrong to bring about the conviction of an innocent person. Therefore, Utilitarianism must be incorrect.

According to the critics of Utilitarianism, this argument illustrates one of the theory's most serious shortcomings, namely, that it is incompatible with the ideal of justice. Justice requires that we treat people fairly, according to the merits of their particular situations. In McCloskey's example, Utilitarianism requires that we treat someone unfairly. Therefore, Utilitarianism cannot be right.

Rights. Here is an example from the U.S. Court of Appeals. In the case of *York v. Story* (1963), arising out of California:

> In October, 1958, appellant [Ms. Angelynn York] went to the police department of Chino for the purpose of filing charges in connection with an assault upon her. Appellee Ron Story, an officer of that police department, then acting under color of his authority as such, advised appellant that it was necessary to take photographs of her. Story then took appellant to a room in the police station, locked the door, and directed her to undress, which she did. Story then directed appellant to assume various indecent positions, and photographed her in those positions. These photographs were not made for any lawful or legitimate purpose.
>
> Appellant objected to undressing. She stated to Story that there was no need to take photographs of her in the nude, or in the positions she was directed to take, because the bruises would not show in any photograph. . . .

Later that month, Story advised appellant that the pictures did not come out and that he had destroyed them. Instead, Story circulated these photographs among the personnel of the Chino police department. In April, 1960, two other officers of that police department, appellee Louis Moreno and defendant Henry Grote, acting under color of their authority as such, and using police photographic equipment located at the police station, made additional prints of the photographs taken by Story. Moreno and Grote then circulated these prints among the personnel of the Chino police department.

Ms. York brought suit against these officers and won. Her legal rights had clearly been violated. But what about the *morality* of the officers' behavior? Utilitarianism says that actions are defensible if they produce a favorable balance of happiness over unhappiness. This suggests that we compare the amount of unhappiness caused to York with the amount of pleasure the photographs gave to Officer Story and the others. And it is at least possible that more happiness than unhappiness was created. In that case, the utilitarian conclusion would be that their actions were morally acceptable. But this seems perverse. Why should the pleasure of Story and his friends matter at all? They had no right to treat York in this way, and the fact that they enjoyed doing so hardly seems relevant.

Consider a related case. Suppose a Peeping Tom spied on a woman through her bedroom window and secretly took pictures of her undressed. Suppose he is never caught, and he never shows the pictures to anyone. Under these circumstances, the only consequence of his action seems to be an increase in his own happiness. No one else, including the woman, is caused any unhappiness at all. How, then, could a utilitarian deny that the Peeping Tom's actions are right? Utilitarianism again appears to be unacceptable.

The key point is that Utilitarianism is at odds with the idea that people have *rights* that may not be trampled on merely because one anticipates good results. In these examples, the woman's right to privacy is violated. But we could think of similar cases in which other rights are at issue—the right to worship freely, the right to speak one's mind, or even the right to live. On Utilitarianism, an individual's rights may always be trampled upon if enough people benefit from the trampling. Utilitarianism has thus been accused of supporting the "tyranny of the majority": if the majority of people would take pleasure in someone's rights being abused, then those rights should be abused, because the pleasure of the majority outweighs the suffering of the one. However, we do not think that our individual rights should mean so little, morally. The notion of an individual right is not a utilitarian notion. Quite the opposite: It is a notion that places limits on how an individual may be treated, regardless of the good that might be accomplished.

Backward-Looking Reasons. Suppose you have promised to do something—say, you promised to meet your friend at a coffee shop this afternoon. But when the time comes to go, you don't want to do it; you need to catch up on some work and you would rather stay home. You try to call her up to cancel, but she isn't answering her cell phone. What should you do? Suppose you judge that the utility of getting your work done slightly outweighs the irritation your friend would experience from being stood up. Applying the utilitarian standard, you might conclude that staying home is better than keeping your promise. However, this does not seem correct. The fact that you *promised* imposes an obligation on you that you cannot escape so easily. Of course, if a great deal were at stake—if, for example, you had to rush your mother to the hospital—you would be justified in breaking the promise. But a *small* gain in happiness cannot overcome the obligation created by your promise; the obligation should mean something, morally. Thus, Utilitarianism once again seems mistaken.

This criticism is possible because Utilitarianism cares only about the *consequences* of our actions. However, we normally think that considerations about the past are important, too. You made a promise to your friend, and that's a fact about the past. Utilitarianism seems faulty because it excludes such backward-looking reasons.

Once we understand this point, we can think of other examples of backward-looking reasons. The fact that someone committed a crime is a reason to punish him. The fact that someone did you a favor last week is a reason for you to do her a favor next week. The fact that you hurt someone yesterday is a reason to make it up to him today. These are all facts about the past that are relevant to determining our obligations. But Utilitarianism makes the past irrelevant, and so it seems flawed.

8.4. Should We Be Equally Concerned for Everyone?

The last part of Utilitarianism says that we must treat each person's happiness as equally important—or as Mill put it, we must be "as strictly impartial as a disinterested and benevolent spectator." Stated abstractly, this sounds plausible, but it has troubling implications. One problem is that the requirement of "equal concern" places too great a demand on us; another problem is that it disrupts our personal relationships.

The Charge That Utilitarianism Is Too Demanding. Suppose you are on your way to the movies when someone points out that the money you are about to spend could be used to feed the starving or to provide inoculations for third-world children. Surely, those people need food and medicine more than you need to see Brad Pitt and Angelina Jolie. So you forgo your entertainment and donate your money to charity. But that is not the end of it. By the same reasoning, you cannot buy new clothes, a car, an iPhone, or a PlayStation. Probably you should move into a cheaper apartment. After all, what's more important— that you have these luxuries, or that children have food?

In fact, faithful adherence to the utilitarian standard would require you to give away your wealth until you've made yourself as poor as the people you're helping. Or rather, you'd need to leave yourself just enough to maintain your job, so that you can keep on giving. Although we would admire someone who did this, we would not think that such a person was merely "doing his duty." Rather, we would regard him as a saint, as someone whose generosity went *beyond* the call of duty. Philosophers call such actions *supererogatory.* But Utilitarianism seems unable to recognize this moral category.

The problem is not merely that Utilitarianism would require us to give away most of our things. It would also prevent us from carrying on our lives. We all have goals and projects that make our lives meaningful. But an ethic that requires us to promote the general welfare would force us to abandon those endeavors. Suppose you are a Web designer, not getting rich but making a decent living; you have two children whom you love; and on weekends, you like to perform with an amateur theater group. In addition, you enjoy reading history. How could there be anything wrong with this? But judged by the utilitarian standard, you are leading an immoral life. After all, you could be doing a lot more good if you spent your time in other ways.

The Charge That Utilitarianism Disrupts Our Personal Relationships. In practice, none of us is willing to treat everyone equally, because that would require giving up our special ties to friends and family. We are all deeply partial where our family and friends are concerned. We love them, and we go to great lengths to help them. To us, they are not just members of the great crowd of humanity—they are special. But all this is inconsistent with impartiality. When you are impartial, you miss out on intimacy, love, affection, and friendship.

At this point, Utilitarianism seems to have lost all touch with reality. What would it be like to care about one's spouse no more than one cares about complete strangers? The very idea is absurd; not only is it profoundly contrary to normal human emotions, but loving relationships could not even exist apart from special responsibilities and obligations. Again, what would it be like to treat one's children with no greater love than one has for strangers? As John Cottingham puts it, "A parent who leaves his child to burn" because "the building contains someone else whose future contribution to the general welfare promises to be greater, is not a hero; he is (rightly) an object of moral contempt, a moral leper."

8.5. The Defense of Utilitarianism

Together, these objections appear to be decisive. Utilitarianism seems unconcerned with both justice and individual rights. Moreover, it cannot account for backward-looking reasons. If we lived by the theory, we would become poor, and we would have to stop loving our family and our friends.

Most philosophers have therefore abandoned Utilitarianism. Some philosophers, however, continue to defend it. They do so in three different ways.

The First Defense: Contesting the Consequences. Most of the arguments against Utilitarianism go like this: a situation is described; then it is said that some particular (vile!) action would have the best consequences under those circumstances; then Utilitarianism is faulted for advocating that action. These arguments, however, succeed only if the actions they describe really would have the best consequences. Would they? According to the first defense, they would not.

Consider, for example, McClosky's argument, in which Utilitarianism is supposed to support framing an innocent man in order to stop a race riot. In the real world, would bearing false witness in this way actually have good consequences? Probably not. The liar might be discovered, and then the situation would be worse than before. And even if the lie succeeded, the real culprit would remain at large and might commit more crimes, to be followed by more riots. Moreover, if the guilty party were later caught, which is always possible, the liar would be in deep trouble, and confidence in the criminal justice system would erode. The moral is that although one might *think* that one can bring about the best consequences by such behavior, experience in fact teaches the opposite: Utility is not served by framing innocent people.

The same goes for the other arguments. Lying, violating people's rights, breaking one's promises, and severing one's intimate relationships all have bad consequences. Only in philosophers' imaginations is it otherwise. In the real world, Peeping Toms are caught, just as Officer Story was caught, and their victims pay the price. In the real world, when people lie, their reputations suffer and other people get hurt; and when people break their promises and fail to return favors, they lose their friends.

So that is the first defense. Unfortunately, it is not very effective. While it is true that *most* acts of false witness and the like have bad consequences, it cannot be said that *all* such acts have bad consequences. At least once in a while, one can bring about a good result by doing something repugnant to moral common sense. Therefore, in at least some real-life cases, Utilitarianism will conflict with common sense. Moreover, even if the anti-utilitarian arguments had to rely on fictitious examples, those arguments would retain their power. Theories like Utilitarianism are supposed to apply to *all* situations, including situations that are merely hypothetical. Thus, showing that Utilitarianism has unacceptable implications in made-up cases is a valid way of critiquing it. The first defense, then, is weak.

The Second Defense: The Principle of Utility Is a Guide for Choosing Rules, Not Acts. Revising a theory is a two-step process: first, you identify which feature of the theory needs work; second, you change only that feature, leaving the rest of the theory intact. What feature of Classical Utilitarianism is causing the trouble?

The troublesome assumption is that *each individual action* should be judged by the utilitarian standard. Whether it would be wrong to tell a particular lie depends on the consequences of *telling that particular lie;* whether you should keep a particular promise depends on the consequences of *keeping that particular promise;* and so on for each of the examples we have considered. If what we care about is the consequences of particular actions, then we can always dream up circumstances in which a horrific action will have the best consequences.

Therefore, the new version of Utilitarianism modifies the theory so that individual actions are no longer judged by the Principle of Utility. Instead, we first ask what *set of rules* is optimal, from a utilitarian viewpoint. In other words, what rules should we follow in order to maximize happiness? Individual acts are then assessed according to whether they abide by these rules. This new version of the theory is called "Rule-Utilitarianism," to distinguish it from the original theory, now commonly called "Act-Utilitarianism."

Rule-Utilitarianism has an easy answer to the anti-utilitarian arguments. An act-utilitarian would incriminate the innocent man in McCloskey's example because the consequences of *that particular act* would be good. But the rule-utilitarian would not reason in that way. She would first ask, What rules of conduct tend to promote the most happiness? And one good rule is "Don't bear false witness against the innocent." That rule is simple and easy to remember, and following it will almost always increase happiness. By appealing to it, the rule-utilitarian can conclude that in McCloskey's example we should not testify against the innocent man.

Similar reasoning can be used to establish rules against violating people's rights, breaking promises, lying, betraying one's friends, and so on. We should accept such rules because following them, as a regular practice, promotes the general happiness. So we no longer judge acts by their utility but by their conformity with these rules. Thus, Rule-Utilitarianism cannot be convicted of violating our moral common sense. In shifting emphasis from the justification of acts to the justification of rules, Utilitarianism has been brought into line with our intuitive judgments.

However, a serious problem with Rule-Utilitarianism arises when we ask whether the ideal rules have *exceptions*. Must the rules be followed no matter what? What if a "forbidden" act would greatly increase the overall good? The rule-utilitarian might give any one of three answers.

First, if she says that in such cases we may violate the rules, then it looks like she wants to assess actions on a case-by-case basis. This is Act-Utilitarianism, not Rule-Utilitarianism.

Second, she might suggest that we formulate the rules so that violating them never will increase happiness. For example, instead of using the rule "Don't bear false witness against the innocent," we might use the rule "Don't bear false witness against the innocent, unless doing so would achieve some great good." If we change all of the rules in this way, then Rule-Utilitarianism will be exactly like Act-Utilitarianism in practice; the rules we follow will always tell us to choose the act that promotes the most happiness. But now Rule-Utilitarianism does not provide a response to the anti-utilitarian arguments; like Act-Utilitarianism, Rule-Utilitarianism tells us to incriminate the innocent, break our promises, spy on people in their homes, and so on.

Finally, the rule-utilitarian might stand her ground and say that we should never break the rules, even to promote happiness. J. J. C. Smart (1920–) says that such a person suffers from an irrational "rule worship." Whatever one thinks of that, this version of Rule-Utilitarianism is not really a utilitarian theory. Utilitarians care solely about happiness and about consequences; but this theory, in addition, cares about following rules. The theory is thus a mix of Utilitarianism and something else entirely. To paraphrase one writer, this type of Rule-Utilitarianism is like a rubber duck: just as a rubber duck is not a kind of duck, this type of Rule-Utilitarianism is not a kind of Utilitarianism. And so, we cannot defend Utilitarianism by appealing to it.

The Third Defense: "Common Sense" Is Wrong. Finally, some utilitarians have offered a very different response to the objections. Upon being told that Utilitarianism conflicts with common sense, they respond, "So what?" Looking back at his own defense of Utilitarianism, J. J. C. Smart writes:

> Admittedly utilitarianism does have consequences which are incompatible with the common moral consciousness, but I tended to take the view "so much the worse for the common moral consciousness." That is, I was inclined to reject the common methodology of testing general ethical principles by seeing how they square with our feelings in particular instances.

This breed of utilitarian—hard-nosed and unapologetic— can offer three responses to the anti-utilitarian arguments.

The First Response: All Values Have a Utilitarian Basis. Critics of Utilitarianism say that the theory can't make sense of some of our most important values—such as the value we attach to truth telling, promise keeping, respecting others' privacy, and loving our children. Consider, for example, lying. The main reason not to lie, the critics say, has nothing to do with bad consequences. The reason is that lying is dishonest; it betrays people's trust. That fact has nothing to do with the utilitarian calculation of benefits. Honesty has a value over and above any value that the utilitarian can acknowledge. And the same is true of promise keeping, respecting others' privacy, and loving our children.

But according to philosophers such as Smart, we should think about these values one at a time and consider why they're important. When people lie, the lies are often discovered, and those betrayed feel hurt and angry. When people break their promises, they irritate their neighbors and alienate their friends. Someone whose privacy is violated may feel humiliated and want to withdraw from others. When people don't care more about their own children than they do about strangers, their children feel unloved, and one day they too may become unloving parents. All these things reduce happiness. Far from being at odds with the idea that we should be honest, dependable, respectful, and loving to our children, Utilitarianism explains why those things are good.

Moreover, apart from the utilitarian explanation, these duties would seem inexplicable. What could be stranger than saying that lying is wrong "in itself," apart from any harm it causes? And how could people have a "right to privacy" unless respecting that right brought them some benefit? On this way of thinking, Utilitarianism is not incompatible with common sense; on the contrary, Utilitarianism justifies the common-sense values we have.

The Second Response: Our Gut Reactions Can't Be Trusted When Cases Are Exceptional. Although some cases of injustice serve the common good, those cases are exceptions. Lying, promise breaking, and violations of privacy usually lead to unhappiness, not happiness. This observation forms the basis of another utilitarian response.

Consider again McCloskey's example of the person tempted to bear false witness. Why do we immediately and instinctively believe it to be wrong to bear false witness against an innocent person? The reason, some say, is that throughout our lives we have seen lies lead to misery and misfortune. Thus, *we instinctively condemn all lies.* But when we condemn lies that are beneficial, our intuitive faculties are misfiring. Experience has taught us to condemn lies because they reduce happiness. Now, however, we are condemning lies that increase happiness. When confronting unusual cases, such as McCloskey's, perhaps we should trust the Principle of Utility more than our gut instincts.

The Third Response: We Should Focus on *All* the Consequences. When we're asked to consider a "despicable" action that maximizes happiness, the action is often presented in a way that encourages us to focus on its bad effects, rather than its good effects. If instead we focus on *all* the effects of the act, Utilitarianism seems more plausible.

Consider yet again the McCloskey example. McCloskey says it would be wrong to convict an innocent man because that would be unjust. But what about the *other* innocent people who will be hurt if the rioting and lynchings continue? What about the pain that will be endured by those who are beaten and tormented by the mob? What about the deaths that will occur if the man doesn't lie? Children will lose their parents, and parents will lose their children. Of course, we never want to face a situation like this. But if we must choose between securing the conviction of one innocent person and allowing the deaths of several innocent people, is it so unreasonable to think that the first option is preferable?

And consider again the objection that Utilitarianism is too demanding because it tells us to use our resources to feed starving children instead of using those resources on ourselves. If we focus our thoughts on those who would starve, do the demands of Utilitarianism seem so unreasonable? Isn't it self-serving of us to say that Utilitarianism is "too demanding," rather than saying that we should do more to help?

This strategy works better for some cases than for others. Consider the Peeping Tom. The unapologetic utilitarian will tell us to consider the pleasure *he* gets from spying on unsuspecting women. If he gets away with it, what harm has been done? Why should his action be condemned? Most people will condemn his behavior, despite the utilitarian arguments. Utilitarianism, as Smart suggests, cannot be fully reconciled with common sense. Whether the theory needs to be reconciled with common sense remains an open question.

8.6. Concluding Thoughts

If we consult what Smart calls our "common moral consciousness," many considerations other than utility seem morally important. But Smart is right to warn us that "common sense" cannot be trusted. That may turn out to be Utilitarianism's greatest contribution. The deficiencies of moral common sense become obvious if we think about it. Many white people once felt that there was an important difference between whites and blacks, so that the interests of whites were somehow more important. Trusting the "common sense" of their day, they might have insisted that an adequate moral theory should accommodate this "fact." Today, no one worth listening to would say such a thing, but who knows how many other irrational prejudices are still part of our moral common sense? At the end of his classic study of race relations, *An American Dilemma*, Nobel Laureate Gunnar Myrdal (1898–1987) reminds us:

> There must be still other countless errors of the same sort that no living man can yet detect, because of the fog within which our type of Western culture envelops us. Cultural influences have set up the assumptions about the mind, the body, and the universe with which we begin; pose the

questions we ask; influence the facts we seek; determine the interpretation we give these facts; and direct our reaction to these interpretations and conclusions.

Could it be, for example, that future generations will look back in disgust at the way affluent people in the 21st century enjoyed their comfortable lives while third-world children died of easily preventable diseases? Or at the way we confined and slaughtered helpless animals? If so, they might note that utilitarian philosophers were ahead of their time in condemning such things.

CHAPTER 9

A *re There Absolute Moral Rules?*

You may not do evil that good may come.
SAINT PAUL, *LETTER TO THE ROMANS* (ca. A.D. 50)

9.1. Harry Truman and Elizabeth Anscombe

Harry S. Truman will always be remembered as the man who made the decision to drop the atomic bombs on Hiroshima and Nagasaki. When he became president in 1945, following the death of Franklin D. Roosevelt, Truman knew nothing about the bomb; Roosevelt's advisors had to fill him in. The Allies were winning the war in the Pacific, they said, but at a terrible cost. Plans had been drawn up for an invasion of Japan, but that battle would be even bloodier than the D-Day assault on Normandy had been. Using the atomic bomb on one or two Japanese cities might bring the war to a speedy end, making the invasion unnecessary.

Truman was at first reluctant to use the new weapon. The problem was that each bomb would obliterate an entire city—not just the military targets, but the hospitals, schools, and homes. Women, children, old people, and other noncombatants would be wiped out along with the military personnel. The Allies had bombed cities before, but Truman sensed that the new weapon made the issue of noncombatants more acute. Moreover, the United States was on record as condemning attacks on civilian targets. In 1939, before America had entered the war, President Roosevelt had sent a message to the governments of France, Germany, Italy, Poland, and Great Britain,

125

denouncing the bombardment of cities in the strongest terms. He had called it an "inhuman barbarism":

> The ruthless bombing from the air of civilians . . . which has resulted in the maiming and in the death of thousands of defenseless men, women, and children, has sickened the hearts of every civilized man and woman, and has profoundly shocked the conscience of humanity. If resort is had to this form of inhuman barbarism during the period of the tragic conflagration with which the world is now confronted, hundreds of thousands of innocent human beings who have no responsibility for, and who are not even remotely participating in, the hostilities which have now broken out, will lose their lives.

Truman expressed similar thoughts when he decided to authorize the bombings. He wrote in his diary that "I have told the Sec. of War, Mr. Stimson, to use it so that military objectives and soldiers and sailors are the target and not women and children. . . . The target will be a purely military one." It is hard to know what to make of this, since Truman knew that the bombs would destroy whole cities. Nonetheless, it is clear that he was worried about the issue of noncombatants.

It is also clear that Truman was sure of his decision. Winston Churchill, the wartime leader of Great Britain, met with Truman shortly before the bombs were dropped, and he later wrote, "The decision whether or not to use the atomic bomb to compel the surrender of Japan was never even an issue. There was unanimous, automatic, unquestioned agreement around our table." After signing the final order, thus sealing the fate of Hiroshima, Truman later said that he "slept like a baby."

Elizabeth Anscombe, who died in 2001, was a 20-year-old student at Oxford University when World War II began. At that time, she co-authored a controversial pamphlet arguing that Britain should not go to war because countries at war inevitably end up fighting by unjust means. "Miss Anscombe," as she was always known—despite her 59-year marriage and her seven children—would go on to become one of the 20th century's most distinguished philosophers, and the greatest woman philosopher in history.

Miss Anscombe was also a Catholic, and her religion was central to her life. Her ethical views reflected traditional Catholic teachings. In 1968, after Pope Paul VI affirmed the church's ban on contraception, she wrote a pamphlet explaining why artificial birth control is immoral. Late in her life, she was arrested while protesting outside a British abortion clinic. She also accepted the church's teaching about the ethical conduct of war, which brought her into conflict with Truman.

Harry Truman and Elizabeth Anscombe crossed paths in 1956. Oxford University was planning to give Truman an honorary degree in thanks for America's wartime help, and those proposing the honor thought it would be uncontroversial. But Anscombe and two other faculty members opposed the idea. Although they lost, they forced a vote on what would otherwise have been a rubber-stamp approval. Then, while the degree was being conferred, Anscombe knelt outside the hall, praying.

Anscombe wrote another pamphlet, this time explaining that Truman was a murderer because he had ordered the bombings of Hiroshima and Nagasaki. Truman, of course, thought the bombings were justified—they had shortened the war and saved lives. For Anscombe, this was not good enough. "For men to choose to kill the innocent as a means to their ends," she wrote, "is always murder." To the argument that the bombings saved more lives than they took, she replied, "Come now: if you had to choose between boiling one baby and letting some frightful disaster befall a thousand people—or a million people, if a thousand is not enough—what would you do?"

Anscombe's example was apt. The bomb blast at Hiroshima, which ignited birds in midair, did lead to babies being boiled: People died in rivers, reservoirs, and cisterns, trying in vain to escape the heat. Anscombe's point was that *some things may not be done, no matter what.* It does not matter if we could accomplish some great good by boiling a baby; it is simply wrong. Anscombe believed in a host of such rules. Under no circumstances, she said, may we intentionally kill innocent people; worship idols; make a false profession of faith; engage in sodomy or adultery; punish one person for the acts of another; or commit treachery, which she describes as "obtaining a man's confidence in a grave matter by promises of trustworthy friendship and then betraying him to his enemies."

Anscombe's husband, Peter Geach (1916–), agreed with this. Anscombe and Geach were the 20th century's foremost philosophical champions of the doctrine that moral rules are absolute.

9.2. The Categorical Imperative

The idea that moral rules have no exceptions is hard to defend. It is easy enough to explain why we *should* break a rule—we can simply point to cases in which following the rule would have terrible consequences. But how can we defend *not* breaking the rule in such cases? It is a daunting assignment. We might say that moral rules are God's inviolable commands. Apart from that, what can be said?

Before the 20th century, there was one major philosopher who believed that moral rules are absolute. Immanuel Kant (1724–1804) argued that lying is wrong under any circumstances. He did not appeal to theological considerations; he held, instead, that reason always forbids lying. To see how he reached this conclusion, we need to look at his general theory of ethics.

Kant observed that the word *ought* is often used nonmorally:

- If you want to become a better chess player, you *ought* to study the games of Garry Kasparov.
- If you want to go to college, you *ought* to take the SAT.

Much of our conduct is governed by such "oughts." The pattern is this: We have a certain desire (to become a better chess player, to go to college); we recognize that a certain course of action will help us get what we want (studying Kasparov's games, taking the SAT); and so we follow the indicated plan.

Kant called these "hypothetical imperatives" because they tell us what to do *provided that* we have the relevant desires. A person who did not want to improve her chess would have no reason to study Kasparov's games; someone who did not want to go to college would have no reason to take the SAT. Because the binding force of the "ought" depends on having the relevant desire, we can escape its force by letting go of the desire. So, for example, I can avoid taking the SAT by deciding that I don't want to go to college.

Moral obligations, by contrast, do not depend on having particular desires. The form of a moral obligation is not "*If* you want so-and-so, then you ought to do such-and-such." Instead, moral requirements are *categorical:* They have the form "You ought to do such-and-such, *period.*" The moral rule is not, for example, that you ought to help people *if* you care about them or *if* you want to be a good person. Instead, the rule is that you should help people *no matter what* your desires are. That is why moral requirements cannot be escaped simply by saying "But I don't care about that."

Hypothetical "oughts" are easy to understand. They merely tell us to do what is necessary to achieve our goals. Categorical "oughts," on the other hand, are mysterious. How can we be obligated to behave in a certain way regardless of our goals? Kant has an answer. Just as hypothetical "oughts" are possible because we have *desires,* categorical "oughts" are possible because we have *reason.* Categorical oughts, Kant says, are derived from a principle that every rational person must accept: the Categorical Imperative. In his *Foundations of the Metaphysics of Morals* (1785), Kant expresses the Categorical Imperative as follows:

> Act only according to that maxim by which you can at the same time will that it should become a universal law.

This principle provides a way to tell whether an act is morally permissible. When you are thinking about doing something, ask what rule you would be following if you actually did it. This rule will be the "maxim" of your act. Then ask whether you would be willing for your maxim to become a universal law. In other words, would you allow your rule to be followed by all people at all times? If so, then your maxim is sound, and your act is acceptable. But if not, then your act is forbidden.

Kant gives several examples of how this works. Suppose, he says, a man needs money, but no one will lend it to him unless he promises to pay it back—which he knows he won't be able to do. Should he make a false promise to get the loan? If he did, his maxim would be: *Whenever you need a loan, promise to repay it, even if you know you can't.* Now, could he will that this rule become a universal law? Obviously not, because it would be self-defeating. Once this rule became a universal practice, no one would believe such promises, and so no one would make loans based on them.

Kant gives another example, about giving aid. Suppose, he says, I refuse to help others in need, saying to myself, "What do I care? Let each person fend for himself." This, again, is a rule that I cannot will to be a universal law. For at some time in the future, I myself will need the help of others, and I will not want them to turn away.

9.3. Kant's Arguments on Lying

According to Kant, then, our behavior should be guided by universal laws, which are moral rules that hold true in all circumstances. Kant believed in many such exceptionless rules. We'll focus on the rule against lying, which Kant had especially strong feelings about. He said that lying under any circumstances is "the obliteration of one's dignity as a human being."

Kant offered two arguments for an absolute rule against lying.

1. His main argument relies on the Categorical Imperative. We could not will a universal law that allows us to lie, Kant said, because such a law would be self-defeating. As soon as lying became common, people would stop believing each other. Lying would then have no point, and in a sense would be impossible, because nobody would pay attention to what you say. Therefore, Kant reasoned, lying cannot be allowed. And so, it is forbidden under any circumstances.

This argument has a flaw, which will become clearer with an example. Suppose it was necessary to lie to save someone's life. Should you do it? Kant would have us reason as follows:

(1) We should do only those actions that conform to rules that we could will to be adopted universally.

(2) If you were to lie, you would be following the rule "It is okay to lie."

(3) This rule could not be adopted universally, because it would be self-defeating: People would stop believing one another, and then it would do no good to lie.

(4) Therefore, you should not lie.

Although Anscombe agreed with Kant's conclusion, she was quick to point out an error in his reasoning. The difficulty arises in step (2). Why should we say that, if you lied, you would be following the rule, "It is okay to lie"? Perhaps your maxim would be: "I will lie when doing so would save someone's life." *That* rule would not be self-defeating. It could become a universal law. And so, by Kant's own theory, it would be all right for you to lie. Thus, Kant's belief that lying is always wrong does not seem to be supported by his own moral theory.

2. Many of Kant's contemporaries thought that his insistence on absolute rules was strange, and they said so. One reviewer challenged him with this example: Imagine that someone is fleeing from a murderer and tells you that he is going home to hide. Then the murderer comes by and asks you where the man is. You believe that, if you tell the truth, you will be aiding in a murder. Furthermore, the killer is already headed the right way, so if you simply remain silent, the worst result is likely. What should you do? Let's call this the Case of the Inquiring Murderer. Under these circumstances, most of us think, you should lie. After all, which is more important: telling the truth or saving someone's life?

Kant responded in an essay with the charmingly old-fashioned title "On a Supposed Right to Lie from Altruistic Motives," in which he gives a second argument against lying. Perhaps, he says, the man on the run has actually left his home, and by telling the truth you would lead the killer to look in the wrong place. However, if you lie, the murderer may wander away and discover the man leaving the area, in which case you would be responsible for his death. Whoever lies, Kant says, "must answer for the consequences, however unforeseeable they were, and pay the penalty for them." Kant states his conclusion in the tone of a stern schoolmaster: "To be truthful . . . in all deliberations, therefore, is a sacred and absolutely commanding decree of reason, limited by no expediency."

This argument may be stated in a general form: We are tempted to make exceptions to the rule against lying because in some cases we think the consequences of honesty will be bad and the consequences of lying will be good. However, we can never be certain about what the consequences will be—we cannot *know* that good results will follow. The results of lying might be unexpectedly bad. Therefore, the best policy is to avoid the known evil—lying—and let the consequences come as they may. Even if the consequences are bad, they will not be our fault, for we will have done our duty.

A similar argument would apply to Truman's decision to drop the atomic bombs on Hiroshima and Nagasaki. The bombs were dropped in the hope that the war could be swiftly concluded. But Truman did not know for sure that this would happen. The Japanese might have hunkered down, and the invasion might still have been necessary. So, Truman was betting hundreds of thousands of lives on the mere hope that good results might ensue.

The problems with this argument are obvious enough—
so obvious, in fact, that it is surprising that a philosopher of
Kant's caliber was not more sensitive to them. In the first place,
the argument depends on an unreasonably pessimistic view of
what we can know. Sometimes we can be quite confident of
what the consequences of our actions will be, in which case we
need not hesitate because of uncertainty. Moreover—and this
is more significant, philosophically—Kant seems to assume that
we would be morally responsible for any bad consequences
of lying, but we would *not* be responsible for any bad consequences of telling the truth. Suppose, as a result of our telling
the truth, the murderer found his victim and killed him. Kant
seems to assume that we would be blameless. But can we escape
responsibility so easily? After all, we aided the murderer. This
argument, then, is not convincing.

Thus, Kant has failed to prove that lying is always wrong.
The Case of the Inquiring Murderer shows what a tough row
he chose to hoe. While Kant believes that any lie "obliterates
one's dignity as a human being," common sense says that some
lies are harmless. In fact, we have a name for them: white lies.
Aren't white lies acceptable—or even required—when they can
be used to save someone's life? This points to the main difficulty for the belief in absolute rules: shouldn't a rule be broken
when following it would be disastrous?

9.4. Conflicts between Rules

Suppose it is held to be absolutely wrong to do X in any circumstances and also wrong to do Y in any circumstances. Then what
about the case in which a person must choose between doing
X and doing Y? This kind of conflict seems to show that moral
rules can't be absolute.

Is there any way that this objection can be met? One way
is to deny that such conflicts ever actually occur. Peter Geach
took this view, appealing to God's providence. We can describe
fictitious cases in which there is no way to avoid violating one
of the absolute rules, he said, but God will not permit such circumstances to arise. Geach writes:

> If God is rational, he does not command the impossible; if
> God governs all events by his providence, he can see to it
> that circumstances in which a man is inculpably faced by

a choice between forbidden acts do not occur. Of course such circumstances . . . are consistently describable; but God's providence could ensure that they do not in fact arise. Contrary to what nonbelievers often say, belief in the existence of God does make a difference to what one expects to happen.

Do such cases actually occur? There is no doubt that serious moral rules sometimes clash. During World War II, Dutch fishermen smuggled Jewish refugees to England in their boats, and sometimes they would be stopped by Nazi patrols. The Nazi captain would call out and ask the Dutch captain where he was going, who was on board, and so forth. The fishermen would lie and be allowed to pass. Clearly, the fishermen had only two options: either they lie, or they let everyone on their boat be killed. No third alternative was available; they could not, for example, remain silent or outrun the Nazis. Thus, Geach appears to have been naïve. Terrible dilemmas do occur in the real world.

If such dilemmas occur, then doesn't this disprove the existence of absolute moral rules? Suppose, for example, the two rules "It is wrong to lie" and "It is wrong to facilitate the murder of innocent people" are both taken to be absolute. The Dutch fishermen would have to do one of these things; therefore, a moral view that absolutely prohibits both is incoherent.

This type of argument is impressive, but it is also limited. It can be levied only against *pairs* of absolute moral rules; two rules are needed to create the conflict. The argument won't stop someone from believing that there is just one absolute rule. And, in a way, everyone does. "Do what is right" is a moral principle we all believe in, which admits of no exceptions. We should always do what is right. However, this rule is so formal that it is trivial—we believe it because it doesn't really say anything. It is not the kind of absolute moral rule that Kant, Geach, and Anscombe wanted to argue for.

9.5. Kant's Insight

Few contemporary philosophers would defend Kant's Categorical Imperative. Yet it might be wrong to dismiss it too quickly. As Alasdair MacIntyre (1929–) observes, "For many who have never heard of philosophy, let alone of Kant, morality is roughly what Kant said it was"—that is, a system of rules that one must follow from a sense of duty. Is there some basic idea underlying the Categorical Imperative that we might accept, even if we don't believe in absolute moral rules? I think there is.

Remember that Kant viewed the Categorical Imperative as binding on rational agents simply because they are rational; in other words, a person who rejected this principle would be guilty not merely of being immoral but also of being irrational. This is a compelling idea. But what exactly does this mean? In what sense would it be irrational to reject the Categorical Imperative?

Note that a moral judgment must be backed by good reasons—if it is true that you ought (or ought not) to do such-and-such, then there must be a reason why you should (or should not) do it. For example, you may think that you ought not to set forest fires because property would be destroyed and people would be killed. The Kantian twist is to point out that *if you accept any considerations as reasons in one case, you must also accept them as reasons in other cases.* If there is another case in which property would be destroyed and people killed, you must accept this as a reason in that case, too. It is no good saying that you can accept reasons some of the time, but not all the time; or that other people must respect them, but not you. Moral reasons, if they are valid at all, are binding on all people at all times. This is a requirement of consistency, and Kant was right to think that no rational person may deny it.

This insight has some important implications. It implies that a person cannot regard herself as special, from a moral point of view: She cannot consistently think that she is permitted to act in ways that are forbidden to others, or that her interests are more important than other people's interests. As one commentator remarked, I cannot say that it is all right for me to drink your beer and then complain when you drink mine. Moreover, it implies that there are rational constraints on what we may do: We may want to do something—say, to drink someone else's beer—but recognize that we cannot consistently do it because we cannot at the same time accept the implication that he may drink our beer. If Kant was not the first to recognize this, he was the first to make it the cornerstone of a fully worked-out system of morals.

But Kant went one step further and said that consistency requires rules that have no exceptions. One can see how his insight pushed him in that direction; but the extra step was not necessary, and it has caused trouble for his theory. Rules, even within a Kantian framework, need not be absolute. All that Kant's basic idea requires is that when we violate a rule, we do so for a reason that we would be willing for anyone to accept. In the Case of the Inquiring Murderer, this means that we may violate the rule against lying only if we would be willing for anyone to lie in the same circumstances. And most of us would readily agree to that.

President Truman could also say that anyone in his position would have been justified in dropping the bomb. Thus, even if Truman was wrong, Kant's arguments do not prove it. One might say that dropping the bomb was wrong because Truman had better options. Perhaps he should have shown the Japanese the power of the bomb by dropping it onto an unpopulated area—negotiations might then have been successful. Or perhaps the Allies could have simply declared victory at that point in the war, even without a Japanese surrender. Saying things like that, however, is very different from saying that what Truman did violated an absolute rule.

CHAPTER 10

Kant and Respect for Persons

Are there any who would not admire man?

GIOVANNI PICO DELLA MIRANDOLA,
ORATION ON THE DIGNITY OF MAN (1486)

10.1. Kant's Core Ideas

Immanuel Kant thought that human beings occupy a special place in creation. Of course, he was not alone in thinking this. From ancient times, humans have considered themselves to be essentially different from all other creatures—and not just different, but better. In fact, humans have traditionally thought themselves to be quite fabulous. Kant certainly did. On his view, human beings have "an intrinsic worth" or "dignity" that makes them valuable "above all price."

Other animals, Kant thought, have value only insofar as they serve human purposes. In his *Lectures on Ethics* (1779), Kant writes, "But so far as animals are concerned, we have no direct duties. Animals . . . are there merely as means to an end. That end is man." We may, therefore, use animals in any way we please. We don't even have a "direct duty" to refrain from torturing them. Kant did condemn the abuse of animals, but not because the animals would be hurt. He worried, rather, about us: "He who is cruel to animals also becomes hard in his dealings with men."

When Kant said that human beings are valuable "above all price," this was not mere rhetoric. Kant meant that people are irreplaceable. If a child dies, this is a tragedy, and it remains tragic even if another child is born into the same family. On the other hand, "mere things" are replaceable. If your printer breaks, then everything is fine so long as you can get another printer. People, Kant believed, have a "dignity" that mere things lack.

Two facts about people, Kant thought, support this judgment.

First, because people have desires, things that satisfy those desires can have value *for* people. By contrast, "mere things" have value only insofar as they promote human ends. Thus, if you want to become a better poker player, a book about poker will have value for you; but apart from such ends, those books are worthless. Or, if you want to go somewhere, a car will have value for you; but apart from such desires, cars have no value.

Mere animals, Kant thought, are too primitive to have self-conscious desires and goals. Thus, they are "mere things." Kant did not believe, for example, that milk has value *for* the cat who wishes to drink it. But today we're more impressed with the mental life of animals than Kant was. We believe that animals do have desires and goals. So, perhaps there are Kantian grounds for saying that animals are not "mere things."

However, Kant's second reason would not apply to animals. People, Kant said, have "an intrinsic worth, i.e., dignity" because they are *rational agents,* that is, free agents capable of making their own decisions, setting their own goals, and guiding their conduct by reason. The only way that moral goodness can exist is for rational creatures *to act from a good will*—that is, to apprehend what they should do and act from a sense of duty. Human beings are the only rational agents that exist on earth; nonhuman animals lack free will, and they do not "guide their conduct by reason," because their rational capacities are too limited. If people disappeared, then so would the moral dimension of the world. This second fact about people is especially important for Kant.

Thus, Kant believed, human beings are not merely one valuable thing among others. Humans are the ones who do the valuing, and it is their conscientious actions that have moral worth. Human beings tower above the realm of things.

These thoughts are central to Kant's moral system. Kant believed that all of our duties can be derived from one ultimate principle, which he called the Categorical Imperative. Kant gave this principle different formulations, but at one point he expresses it like this:

> Act so that you treat humanity, whether in your own person or in that of another, always as an end and never as a means only.

Because people are so valuable, morality requires us to treat them "always as an end and never as a means only." What does this mean, and why should anyone believe it?

To treat people "as an end" means, on the most superficial level, treating them well. We must promote their welfare, respect their rights, avoid harming them, and generally "endeavor, so far as we can, to further the ends of others." But Kant's idea also has a deeper implication. To treat people as ends requires treating them with respect. Thus, we may not manipulate people, or "use" people to achieve our goals, no matter how good those goals may be. Kant gives this example: Suppose you need money, and you want a loan, but you know you cannot repay it. In desperation, you consider telling your friend you will repay it in order to get the money. May you do this? Perhaps you need the money for a good purpose—so good, in fact, that you might convince yourself that the lie would be justified. Nevertheless, you should not lie to your friend. If you did, you would be manipulating her and using her "merely as a means."

On the other hand, what would it be like to treat your friend "as an end"? Suppose you tell the truth—you tell her why you need the money, and you tell her you won't be able to pay her back. Then your friend can make up her own mind about whether to give you the loan. She can consult her own values and wishes, exercise her own powers of reasoning, and make a free choice. If she then decides to give you the money for your stated purpose, she will be choosing *to make that purpose her own.* Thus, you will not be using her as a mere means to achieving your goal, for it will be her goal, too. Thus, for Kant, to treat people as ends is to treat them "as beings who [can] contain in themselves the end of the very same action."

When you tell your friend the truth, and she gives you money, you are using her as a means to getting the money. However, Kant does not object to treating someone as a means; he objects to treating someone *only* as a means. Consider another example: Suppose your bathroom sink is stopped up. Would it be okay to call in a plumber—to "use" the plumber as a means to unclogging the drain? Kant would have no problem with this. The plumber, after all, understands the situation. You are not deceiving or manipulating him. He may freely choose to unclog your drain in exchange for payment. Although you are treating the plumber as a means, you are also treating him with dignity, as an "end-in-himself."

Treating people as ends, and respecting their rational capacities, has other implications. We should not force adults to do things against their will; instead, we should let them make their own decisions. We should therefore be wary of laws that aim to protect people from themselves—for example, laws requiring people to wear seat belts or motorcycle helmets. Also, we shouldn't forget that respecting *people* requires respecting *ourselves*. I should take good care of myself; I should develop my talents; I should do more than just slide by.

Kant's moral system is not easy to grasp. To understand it better, let's consider how Kant applied his ideas to the practice of criminal punishment. The rest of this chapter is devoted to that example.

10.2. Retribution and Utility in the Theory of Punishment

Jeremy Bentham (1748–1832) said that "all punishment is mischief: all punishment in itself is evil." Bentham had a point. Punishment, by its nature, always involves inflicting some harm on the person punished. As a society, we punish people by making them pay fines or go to prison, or even, sometimes, by killing them. How can it be right to treat people in these ways?

The traditional answer is that punishment is justified as a way of "paying back" the offender for his wicked deed. Those who have committed a crime deserve to be treated badly. It is a matter of justice: If you harm other people, justice requires that you be harmed, too. As the ancient saying has it, "An eye for an eye, and a tooth for a tooth." According to the doctrine of Retributivism, this is the main justification of punishment.

Retributivism was, on Bentham's view, a wholly unsatisfactory idea, because it advocates the infliction of suffering without any compensating gain in happiness. Retributivism would have us increase, not decrease, the amount of misery in the world. Kant was a retributivist, and he openly embraced this implication. In *The Critique of Practical Reason* (1788), he writes:

> When someone who delights in annoying and vexing peace-loving folk receives at last a right good beating, it is

certainly an ill, but everyone approves of it and considers
it as good in itself even if nothing further results from it.

Thus, punishing people may increase the amount of misery in
the world; but that is all right, for the extra suffering is borne
by those who deserve it.

Utilitarianism takes a very different approach. According to
Utilitarianism, our duty is to do whatever will increase the amount
of happiness in the world. Punishment is, on its face, "an evil"
because it makes the punished person unhappy. Thus, Bentham,
a utilitarian, says, "If [punishment] ought at all to be admitted,
it ought to be admitted in as far as it promises to exclude some
greater evil." In other words, punishment can be justified only if
it does enough good to outweigh the bad. And utilitarians have
traditionally thought that it does. If someone breaks the law,
then punishing that person can have several benefits.

First, punishment provides comfort and gratification to
victims and their families. People feel very strongly that someone who mugged, raped, or robbed them should not go free.
Victims also live in fear when they know that their attacker has
not been caught. Philosophers sometimes ignore this justification of punishment, but it plays a prominent role in our legal
system. Judges, lawyers, and juries often want to know what victims want. Indeed, whether the police will make an arrest, and
whether the district attorney's office will prosecute a case, often
depends on the wishes of the victims.

Second, by locking up criminals, or by executing them, we
take them off the street. With fewer criminals on the street, there
will be less crime. In this way, prisons protect society and thus
reduce unhappiness. Of course, this justification does not apply
to punishments in which the offender remains free, such as when
a criminal is sentenced to probation with community service.

Third, punishment reduces crime by deterring would-be
criminals. Someone who is tempted to commit a crime might
not do so if he knows he might be punished. Obviously, the
threat of punishment is not always effective; sometimes people
break the law anyway. But there will be *less* misconduct if punishments are threatened. Imagine what would happen if the
police stopped arresting thieves; surely there would be a lot
more theft. Deterring crime thus prevents unhappiness.

Fourth, a well-designed system of punishment might help
to rehabilitate wrongdoers. Criminals often have mental and

emotional problems. Often, they are uneducated and illiterate and cannot hold down jobs. Why not respond to crime by attacking the problems that cause it? If someone is dangerous, we may imprison him. But while we have him behind bars, why not address his problems with psychological therapy, educational opportunities, and job training? If one day he can return to society as a productive citizen, then both he and society will benefit.

In America, the utilitarian view of punishment was once dominant. In 1954, the American Prison Association changed its name to "the American Correctional Association" and encouraged prisons to become "correctional facilities." Prisons were thus asked to "correct" inmates, not to "punish" them. Prison reform was common in the 1950s and 1960s. Prisons offered their inmates drug treatment programs, vocational training classes, and group counseling sessions, hoping to turn them into good citizens.

Those days, however, are long gone. In the 1970s, the newly announced "war on drugs" led to longer and longer prison sentences for drug offenders. This change in American justice was more retributive than utilitarian in nature, and it resulted in vastly more prisoners. Today the United States houses around 2.3 million inmates, giving it the highest incarceration rate of any country, by far. Most of those inmates are in state prisons, not federal prisons, and the states that must operate those facilities are strapped for cash. As a result, most of the programs aimed at rehabilitation were either scaled back or eliminated. The rehabilitation mentality of the 1960s has thus been replaced by a warehousing mentality, marked by prison overcrowding and plagued by underfunding. This new reality, which is less pleasant for the inmates themselves, suggests a victory for Retributivism.

10.3. Kant's Retributivism

The utilitarian theory of punishment has many opponents. Some critics say that prison reform does not work. California had the most vigorous program of reform in the United States, yet its prisoners were especially likely to commit crimes after being released. Most of the opposition, however, is based on theoretical considerations that go back at least to Kant.

Kant despised "the serpent-windings of Utilitarianism" because, he said, the theory is incompatible with human dignity. In the first place, it has us calculating how to use people as means to our ends. If we imprison the criminal in order to keep society safe, we are merely using him for the benefit of others. This violates Kant's belief that "one man ought never to be dealt with merely as a means subservient to the purpose of another."

Moreover, rehabilitation is really just the attempt to mold people into what *we* want them to be. As such, it violates their right to decide for themselves what sort of people they will be. We do have the right to respond to their wickedness by "paying them back" for it, but we do not have the right to violate their integrity by trying to manipulate their personalities.

Thus, Kant would have no part of utilitarian justifications. Instead, he argues that punishment should be governed by two principles. First, people should be punished simply because they have committed crimes, and for no other reason. Second, punishment should be *proportionate* to the seriousness of the crime. Small punishments may suffice for small crimes, but big punishments are necessary for big crimes:

> But what is the mode and measure of punishment which public justice takes as its principle and standard? It is just the principle of equality, by which the pointer of the scale of justice is made to incline no more to the one side than to the other. . . . Hence it may be said: "If you slander another, you slander yourself; if you steal from another, you steal from yourself; if you strike another, you strike yourself; if you kill another, you kill yourself." This is . . . the only principle which . . . can definitely assign both the quality and the quantity of a just penalty.

Kant's second principle leads him to endorse capital punishment; for in response to murder, only death is appropriate. In a famous passage, Kant says:

> Even if a civil society resolved to dissolve itself with the consent of all its members—as might be supposed in the case of a people inhabiting an island resolving to separate and scatter throughout the whole world—the last murderer lying in prison ought to be executed before the resolution was carried out. This ought to be done in order that

everyone may realize the desert of his deeds, and that blood-guiltiness may not remain on the people; for otherwise they will all be regarded as participants in the murder as a public violation of justice.

Although a Kantian must support the death penalty *in theory*, she might oppose it *in practice*. The worry, in practice, is that innocent people might be killed by mistake. In the United States, around 130 death row inmates have been released from prison after being proved innocent. None of those people were actually killed. But with so many close calls, it is almost certain that some innocent people have been put to death—and advocates of reform point to specific, troubling examples. Thus, in deciding whether to support a policy of capital punishment, Kantians must balance the injustice of the occasional, deadly mistake against the injustice of letting killers live.

Kant's two principles describe a general theory of punishment: Wrongdoers must be punished, and the punishment must fit the crime. This theory is deeply opposed to the Christian idea of turning the other cheek. In the Sermon on the Mount, Jesus avows, "You have heard that it was said, 'An eye for an eye and a tooth for a tooth.' But I say to you, Do not resist the one who is evil. If anyone slaps you on the right cheek, turn to him the other also." For Kant, such a response to evil is not only imprudent, but unjust.

What arguments can be given for Kant's Retributivism? We noted that Kant regards punishment as a matter of justice. He says that if the guilty are not punished, justice is not done. That is one argument. Also, we discussed why Kant rejects the utilitarian view of punishment. But he also provides another argument, based on his idea of treating people as "ends-in-themselves." This additional argument is Kant's contribution to the theory of Retributivism.

On the face of it, it seems unlikely that we could describe punishing someone as "respecting him as a person" or as "treating him as an end." How could sending someone to prison be a way of respecting him? Even more paradoxically, how could executing someone be a way of treating him with dignity? For Kant, treating someone "as an end" means treating him as a rational being, who is responsible for his behavior. So now we may ask: What does it mean to be a responsible being?

Consider, first, what it means *not* to be such a being. Mere animals, who lack reason, are not responsible for their actions; nor are people who are mentally ill and not in control of themselves. In such cases, it would be absurd to "hold them accountable." We could not properly feel gratitude or resentment toward them, because they are not responsible for any good or ill they cause. Moreover, we cannot expect them to understand *why* we treat them as we do, any more than they understand why they behave as they do. So we have no choice but to deal with them by manipulating them, rather than by treating them as rational individuals. When we scold a dog for eating off the table, for example, we are merely trying to "train" him.

On the other hand, a rational being can freely decide what to do, based on his own conception of what is best. Rational beings *are* responsible for their behavior, and so they are accountable for what they do. We may feel gratitude when they behave well and resentment when they behave badly. Reward and punishment—not "training" or other manipulation—are the natural expressions of gratitude and resentment. Thus, in punishing people, we are holding them responsible for their actions in a way in which we cannot hold mere animals responsible. We are responding to them not as people who are "sick" or who have no control over themselves, but as people who have freely chosen their evil deeds.

Furthermore, in dealing with responsible agents, we may properly allow their conduct to determine, at least in part, how we respond to them. If someone has been kind to you, you may respond by being generous; and if someone is nasty to you, you may take that into account in deciding how to respond. And why shouldn't you? Why should you treat everyone alike, regardless of how *they* have chosen to behave?

Kant gives this last point a distinctive twist. There is, on his view, a deep reason for responding to other people "in kind." When we choose to do something, after consulting our own values, we are in effect saying *this is the sort of thing that should be done.* In Kant's terminology, we are implying that our conduct be made into a "universal law." Therefore, when a rational being decides to treat people in a certain way, he decrees that in his judgment *this is the way people are to be treated.* Thus, if we treat him the same way in return, we are doing nothing more than treating him *as he has decided that people are to be treated.* If he treats others badly, and we treat him badly, we are complying with his own decision. We are, in a perfectly clear sense, respecting his judgment, by allowing it to control how we treat him. Thus, Kant says of the criminal, "His own evil deed draws the punishment upon himself."

This last argument can certainly be questioned. Why should we adopt the criminal's principle of action, rather than follow our own principles? Shouldn't we try to be "better than he is"? At the end of the day, what we think of Kant's theory may depend on our view of criminal behavior. If we see criminals as victims of circumstance, who do not ultimately control their own actions, then the utilitarian model will appeal to us. On the other hand, if we see criminals as rational agents who freely choose to do harm, then Kantian Retributivism will have great appeal for us. The resolution of this great debate might thus turn on whether we believe that human beings have free will, or whether we believe that outside forces impact human behavior so deeply that our freedom is an illusion. The debate about free will, however, is so complex, and so concerned with matters outside of ethics, that we will not discuss it here. This kind of dialectical situation is common in philosophy: when you study one matter deeply, you often come to realize that it depends on something else. And, unfortunately, that other thing often turns out to be as difficult as the set of problems you began with.

CHAPTER 11

Feminism and the Ethics of Care

> But it is obvious that the values of women differ very often from the values which have been made by the other sex; naturally, this is so. Yet it is the masculine values that prevail.
>
> VIRGINIA WOOLF, *A ROOM OF ONE'S OWN* (1929)

11.1. Do Women and Men Think Differently about Ethics?

The idea that women and men think differently has traditionally been used to justify discrimination against women. Aristotle said that women are not as rational as men, and so they are naturally ruled by men. Immanuel Kant agreed, adding that women "lack civil personality" and should have no voice in public life. Jean-Jacques Rousseau tried to put a good face on this by emphasizing that women and men merely possess different virtues; but, of course, it turned out that men's virtues fit them for leadership, whereas women's virtues fit them for home and hearth.

Against this background, it is not surprising that the women's movement of the 1960s and 1970s denied that women and men differ psychologically. The conception of men as rational and women as emotional was dismissed as a mere stereotype. Nature makes no mental or moral distinction between the sexes, it was said; and when there seem to be differences, it is only because women have been conditioned by an oppressive system to behave in "feminine" ways.

These days, however, most feminists believe that women do think differently than men. But, they add, women's ways of thinking are not inferior to men's, nor do the differences justify

146

any kind of prejudice. On the contrary, female ways of thinking yield insights that have been missed in male-dominated areas. Thus, by attending to the distinctive approach of women, we can make progress in subjects that were stalled. Ethics is said to be a leading candidate for this treatment.

Kohlberg's Stages of Moral Development. Consider the following problem, devised by the educational psychologist Lawrence Kohlberg (1927–1987). Heinz's wife was near death, and her only hope was a drug that had been discovered by a pharmacist who was now selling it for an outrageously high price. The drug cost $200 to make, and the pharmacist was selling it for $2,000. Heinz could raise only half of that. The pharmacist said that half wasn't enough, and when Heinz promised to pay the rest later, the pharmacist still refused. In desperation, Heinz considered stealing the drug. Would that be wrong?

This problem, known as "Heinz's Dilemma," was used by Kohlberg in studying the moral development of children. Kohlberg interviewed children of various ages, presenting them with a series of dilemmas and asking them questions designed to reveal their thinking. Analyzing their responses, Kohlberg concluded that there are six stages of moral development. In these stages, the child or adult conceives of "right" in terms of

> obeying authority and avoiding punishment (stage 1);
>
> satisfying one's own desires and letting others do the same, through fair exchanges (stage 2);
>
> cultivating one's relationships and performing the duties of one's social roles (stage 3);
>
> obeying the law and maintaining the welfare of the group (stage 4);
>
> upholding the basic rights and values of one's society (stage 5);
>
> abiding by abstract, universal moral principles (stage 6).

So, if all goes well, we begin life with a self-centered desire to avoid punishment, and we end life with a set of abstract moral principles. Kohlberg, however, believed that only a small minority of adults make it to stage 5.

Heinz's Dilemma was presented to an 11-year-old boy named Jake, who thought it was obvious that Heinz should steal the drug. Jake explained:

> For one thing, a human life is worth more than money, and if the druggist only makes $1,000, he is still going to live, but if Heinz doesn't steal the drug, his wife is going to die.
>   *(Why is life worth more than money?)*
>   Because the druggist can get a thousand dollars later from rich people with cancer, but Heinz can't get his wife again.
>   *(Why not?)*
>   Because people are all different and so you couldn't get Heinz's wife again.

But Amy, also 11, saw the matter differently. Should Heinz steal the drug? Compared to Jake, Amy seems hesitant and evasive:

> Well, I don't think so. I think there might be other ways besides stealing it, like if he could borrow the money or make a loan or something, but he really shouldn't steal the drug—but his wife shouldn't die either. . . . If he stole the drug, he might save his wife then, but if he did, he might have to go to jail, and then his wife might get sicker again, and he couldn't get more of the drug, and it might not be good. So, they should really just talk it out and find some other way to make the money.

The interviewer asks Amy further questions, but she will not budge; she refuses to accept the terms in which the problem is posed. Instead, she recasts the issue as a conflict between Heinz and the pharmacist that must be resolved by further discussions.

In terms of Kohlberg's stages, Jake seems to have advanced beyond Amy. Amy's response is typical of people operating at stage 3, where personal relationships are paramount—Heinz and the pharmacist must work things out between them. Jake, on the other hand, appeals to impersonal principles—"a human life is worth more than money." Jake seems to be operating at one of the later stages.

Gilligan's Objection. Kohlberg began studying moral development in the 1950s. Back then, psychologists almost always studied behavior rather than thought processes, and psychological researchers were thought of as men in white coats who watched rats run through mazes. Kohlberg's humanistic, cognitive approach pursued knowledge in a more appealing way. However, his central idea was flawed. It is legitimate to study how people think at different ages—if children think differently at ages 5, 10, and 15, that is certainly worth knowing about. It is also worthwhile to identify the best ways of thinking. But these projects are different. One involves observing how children, in fact, think; the other involves assessing ways of thinking as better or worse. Different kinds of evidence are relevant to each investigation, and there is no reason to assume in advance that the results will match. Contrary to the opinion of older people, it *could* turn out that age does not bring wisdom.

Kohlberg's theory has also been criticized from a feminist perspective. In 1982, Carol Gilligan wrote a book called *In a Different Voice,* in which she objects to what Kohlberg says about Jake and Amy. The two children think differently, she says, but Amy's way of thinking is not inferior. When confronted with Heinz's Dilemma, Amy responds to the personal aspects of the situation, as females typically do, whereas Jake, thinking like a male, sees only "a conflict between life and property that can be resolved by a logical deduction." Jake's response will be judged "at a higher level" only if one assumes, as Kohlberg does, that an ethic of principle is superior to an ethic of intimacy and caring. But why should we assume that? Admittedly, most moral philosophers have favored an ethic of principle, but that may be because most moral philosophers have been men.

The "male way of thinking"—the appeal to impersonal principles—abstracts away the details that give each situation its special flavor. Women, Gilligan says, find it harder to ignore those details. Amy worries, "If [Heinz] stole the drug, he might save his wife then, but if he did, he might have to go to jail, and then his wife might get sicker again, and he couldn't get more of the drug." Jake, who reduces the situation to "a human life is worth more than money," ignores all this.

Gilligan suggests that women's basic moral orientation is one of caring: "taking care" of others in a personal way, not just being concerned for humanity in general. This explains why Amy's response seems, at first, confused and uncertain. Sensitivity to the needs of others leads women to "attend to voices other than their own and to include in their judgment other points of view." Thus, Amy could not simply reject the pharmacist's point of view; rather, she wanted to talk to him and try to accommodate him. According to Gilligan, "Women's moral weakness, manifest in an apparent diffusion and confusion of judgment, is thus inseparable from women's moral strength, an overriding concern with relationships and responsibilities."

Other feminists have taken these ideas and molded them into a distinctive view of ethics. Virginia Held (1929–) sums up the central idea: "Caring, empathy, feeling with others, being sensitive to each other's feelings, all may be better guides to what morality requires in actual contexts than may abstract rules of reason, or rational calculation, or at least they may be necessary components of an adequate morality."

Before discussing this idea, we may pause to consider how "feminine" it really is. *Do* women and men think differently about ethics? And if they do, why do they?

Is It True That Women and Men Think Differently? Since Gilligan's book appeared, psychologists have conducted hundreds of studies on gender, the emotions, and morality. These studies reveal some differences between women and men. Women tend to score higher than men on tests that measure empathy. Also, brain scans reveal that women have a lower tendency than men to enjoy seeing people punished who have treated them unfairly—perhaps because women empathize even with those who have wronged them. Finally, women seem to care more about close personal relationships, whereas men care more about larger networks of shallow relationships. As Roy Baumeister put it, "Women specialize in the narrow sphere of intimate relationships. Men specialize in the larger group."

Women and men probably do think differently about ethics. These differences, however, cannot be very great. It is not as though women make judgments that are incomprehensible to men, or vice versa. Men can understand the value of caring relationships, even if they have to be reminded sometimes; and they can agree with Amy that the happiest solution to Heinz's Dilemma would be for the two men to work it out. For their part, women will hardly disagree that human life is worth more than money. And when we look at individuals, we find that some men are especially caring, while some women rely heavily on abstract principles. Plainly, the two sexes do not inhabit different moral universes. One scholarly article reviewed 180 studies and found that women are only slightly more care-oriented than men, and men are only slightly more justice-oriented than women. Even this watered-down conclusion, however, invites the question: Why should women be, on average, more caring than men?

There seem to be two possibilities. First, we might look for a social explanation. Perhaps women care more because of the social roles they occupy. Traditionally, women have been expected to do the housework and take care of the kids. Even if this expectation is sexist, the fact remains that women have often performed these functions. And it is easy to see how taking care of a family could lead one to adopt an ethic of care. Thus, the care perspective could be part of the psychological conditioning that girls receive.

On the other hand, we might seek a genetic explanation. Some differences between males and females show up at a very early age. One-year-old girls will spend more time looking at a film of a face than a film of cars, whereas one-year-old boys prefer the cars. Even one-day-old girls, but not one-day-old boys, will spend more time looking at a friendly face than looking at a mechanical object of the same size. This suggests that females might naturally be more social than males. If this were true, why would it be true?

Charles Darwin's theory of evolution might provide some insight. We may think of the Darwinian "struggle for survival" as a competition to get the maximum number of one's genes into the next generation. Traits that help accomplish this will be preserved in future generations, while traits that work against this goal will tend to disappear. In the 1970s, researchers in the field of Evolutionary Psychology began applying these ideas to human psychology. The idea is that people today have the emotions and behavioral tendencies that enabled their ancestors to survive and reproduce in the distant past.

From this point of view, the key difference between males and females is that men can father thousands of children, while women can give birth only once every nine and a half months, until menopause. This means that males and females have different reproductive strategies. For men, the optimum strategy is to impregnate as many women as possible. Having done that, the man cannot devote much time to any particular child. For women, the optimum strategy is to invest heavily in each child and to have sex only with those men who are willing to stick around. This creates a tension between men and women, and it might explain why the sexes have evolved different attitudes. It explains, notoriously, why men have a greater sex drive than women. It also explains why women might be more attracted than men to the values of the nuclear family—in particular, to the value of caring.

This kind of explanation is often misunderstood. The point is not that people consciously calculate how to propagate their genes; no one does that. Nor is the point that people *should* calculate in this way; from an ethical point of view, they should not. The point is just to explain what we observe.

11.2. Implications for Moral Judgment

Not all female philosophers are feminists, and not all feminists embrace the ethics of care. Nonetheless, the ethics of care is closely identified with modern feminist philosophy. As Annette Baier (1929–) puts it, "'Care' is the new buzzword."

One way of understanding an ethical view is to ask what difference it would make in practice. Does an ethic of care have different implications than a "male" approach to ethics? Here are three examples.

Family and Friends. Traditional theories of obligation are notoriously ill-suited to describing life among family and friends. Those theories take the notion of *what we should do* as morally fundamental. But, as Baier observes, when we try to construe "being a loving parent" as a duty, we encounter problems. A loving parent is motivated by love, not by duty. If parents care for their children only because they feel it is their duty, the children will sense it and realize they are unloved.

Moreover, the ideas of equality and impartiality that pervade theories of obligation seem deeply antagonistic to the values of love and friendship. John Stuart Mill (1806–1873) said that a moral agent must be "as strictly impartial as a disinterested and benevolent spectator." But that is not the standpoint of a parent or friend. We do not regard our family and friends merely as members of the great crowd of humanity; we think of them as special.

The ethics of care, on the other hand, is perfectly suited to describe such relations. The ethics of care does not take "obligation" or "duty" as fundamental; nor does it require that we impartially promote the interests of everyone alike. Instead, it begins with a conception of moral life as a network of relationships with specific people, and it sees "living well" as caring for those people, attending to their needs, and maintaining their trust.

These outlooks lead to different judgments about what we may do. May I devote my time and resources to caring for my friends and family, even if this means ignoring the needs of other people? From an impartial point of view, our duty is to promote the interests of everyone alike. But few of us accept that view. The ethics of care affirms the priority that we naturally give to our family and friends, and so it seems more plausible than an ethic of principle. Of course, it is not surprising that the ethics of care appears to do a good job of explaining the nature of our moral relations with friends and family. After all, those relationships are its primary inspiration.

Children with HIV. Around the world, about 2.5 million children under the age of 15 have HIV, the virus that can cause AIDS. Right now only one-fourth of those children get decent medical care, while only half of pregnant women who have HIV are taking steps to protect their unborn children from the virus. Organizations such as UNICEF work to improve these numbers, but they never have enough money. By contributing to their work, we could save lives.

A traditional ethic of principle, such as Utilitarianism, would conclude from this that we have a substantial duty to support UNICEF. The reasoning is straightforward: Almost all of us spend money on luxuries. Luxuries are not as important as protecting children from AIDS. Therefore, we should give at least some of our money to UNICEF. Of course, this argument would become complicated if we tried to fill in all the details. But the basic idea is clear enough.

One might think that an ethic of care would reach a similar conclusion—after all, shouldn't we care for those disadvantaged children? But that misses the point. An ethic of care focuses on small-scale, personal relationships. If there is no such relationship, "caring" cannot take place. Nel Noddings (1929–) explains that the caring relation can exist only if the "cared-for" can interact with the "one-caring." At a minimum, the cared-for must be able to receive and acknowledge the care in a personal, one-to-one encounter. Otherwise, there is no obligation: "We are not obliged to act as one-caring if there is no possibility of completion in the other." Thus, Noddings concludes that we have no obligation to help "the needy in the far regions of the earth."

Many feminists regard Noddings's view as too extreme. Making personal relationships the whole of ethics, as she does, seems as wrong-headed as ignoring them altogether. A better approach might be to say that the ethical life includes both caring relationships *and* a benevolent concern for people generally. Our obligation to support UNICEF might then be seen as arising from our obligations of benevolence. If we take this approach, we may interpret the ethics of care as *supplementing* traditional theories rather than replacing them. Annette Baier seems to have this in mind when she writes that, eventually, "women theorists will need to connect their ethics of love with what has been the men theorists' preoccupation, namely, obligation."

Animals. Do we have obligations to nonhuman animals? Should we, for example, refrain from eating them? One argument from an ethic of principle says that how we raise animals for food causes them great suffering, and so we should nourish ourselves without the cruelty. Since the modern animal rights movement began in the 1970s, this sort of argument has persuaded many people to become vegetarians.

Noddings suggests that this is a good issue "to test the basic notions on which an ethic of caring rests." What are those basic notions? First, such an ethic appeals to intuition and feeling rather than to principle. This leads to a different conclusion about vegetarianism, for most people do not feel that eating meat is wrong or that the suffering of livestock is important. Noddings observes that our emotional responses to humans are different from our responses to animals.

A second "basic notion on which an ethic of caring rests" is the primacy of personal relationships. These relationships, as we have noted, always involve the cared-for interacting with the one-caring. Noddings believes that people do have this sort of relationship with their pets:

> When one is familiar with a particular animal family, one comes to recognize its characteristic form of address. Cats, for example, lift their heads and stretch toward the one they are addressing. . . . When I enter my kitchen in the morning and my cat greets me from her favorite spot on the counter, I understand her request. This is the spot where she sits and "speaks" in her squeaky attempt to communicate her desire for a dish of milk.

A relationship is established, and the attitude of care must be summoned. But one has no such relationship with the cow in the slaughterhouse, and so, Noddings concludes, we have no obligation not to eat it.

What are we to make of this? If we use this issue "to test the basic notions on which an ethic of caring rests," does the ethic pass or fail the test? The opposing arguments are impressive. First, intuition and feeling are not reliable guides—at one time, people's intuitions told them that slavery was acceptable and that the subordination of women to men was God's plan. And second, whether the animal is in a position to respond "personally" to you may have a lot to do with the satisfaction you get from helping, but it has nothing to do with the animal's needs. Similarly, whether a faraway child would suffer from being HIV+ has nothing to do with whether she can thank you personally for helping her avoid infection. These arguments, of course, appeal to principles that are said to be typical of male reasoning. Therefore, if the ethic of care is taken to be the whole of morality, such arguments will be ignored. On the other hand, if caring is only one part of morality, the arguments from principle will have considerable force. Livestock might come within the sphere of moral concern, not because of our caring relation with them, but for other reasons.

11.3. Implications for Ethical Theory

It is easy to see the influence of men's experience in the ethical theories they have created. Historically, men have dominated public life, where relationships are often impersonal and contractual. In politics and business, relationships can even be adversarial when interests collide. So we negotiate; we bargain and make deals. Moreover, in public life our decisions may affect large numbers of people we do not know. So we may try to calculate which decisions will have the best overall outcome for the most people. And what do men's theories emphasize? Impersonal duty, contracts, the balancing of competing interests, and the calculation of costs and benefits.

Little wonder, then, that feminists accuse moral philosophy of having a male bias. The concerns of private life are almost wholly absent, and the "different voice" of which Carol Gilligan speaks is silent. A moral theory tailored to women's concerns would look very different. In the small-scale world of friends and family, bargaining and calculating play a much smaller role, while love and caring dominate. Once this point is made, there is no denying that morality must find a place for it.

Private life, however, is not easy to accommodate within the traditional theories. As we noted, "being a loving parent" is not about calculating how one should behave. The same might be said about being a loyal friend or a dependable coworker. To be loving, loyal, and dependable is to be *a certain kind of person,* which is very different from impartially "doing your duty."

The contrast between "being a certain kind of person" and "doing your duty" lies at the heart of a larger conflict between two kinds of ethical theory. Virtue Ethics sees being a moral person as having certain traits of character: being kind, generous, courageous, just, prudent, and so on. Theories of obligation, on the other hand, emphasize impartial duty: They portray the moral agent as someone who listens to reason, figures out the right thing to do, and does it. One of the chief arguments for Virtue Ethics is that it seems well suited to accommodate the values of both public and private life. The two spheres simply require different virtues. Public life requires justice and beneficence, while private life requires love and caring.

The ethics of care, therefore, may be best understood as one part of the ethics of virtue. Many feminist philosophers view it in this light. Although Virtue Ethics is not an exclusively feminist project, it is so closely tied to feminist ideas that Annette Baier dubs its male promoters "honorary women." The verdict on the ethics of care may depend, ultimately, on the viability of a broader theory of the virtues.

CHAPTER 12

Virtue Ethics

The excellency of hogs is fatness, of men virtue.
                    BENJAMIN FRANKLIN, *POOR RICHARD'S ALMANACK* (1736)

12.1. The Ethics of Virtue and the Ethics of Right Action

In thinking about any subject, it matters greatly what questions we start with. In Aristotle's *Nicomachean Ethics* (ca. 325 B.C.), the central questions are about *character*. Aristotle begins by asking "What is the good of man?" and his answer is "an activity of the soul in conformity with virtue." He then discusses such virtues as courage, self-control, generosity, and truthfulness. Most of the ancient thinkers came to ethics by asking *What traits of character make someone a good person?* As a result, "the virtues" occupied center stage in their discussions.

As time passed, however, this way of thinking became neglected. With the coming of Christianity, a new set of ideas emerged. The Christians, like the Jews, viewed God as a lawgiver, and so they saw obedience to those laws as the key to righteous living. For the Greeks, the life of virtue was inseparable from the life of reason. But Saint Augustine, the influential fourth-century Christian thinker, distrusted reason and believed that moral goodness depends on subordinating oneself to the will of God. Thus, when medieval philosophers discussed the virtues, it was in the context of Divine Law, and the "theological virtues" of faith, hope, charity, and obedience occupied the spotlight.

After the Renaissance period (1400–1650), moral philosophy again became more secular, but philosophers did not return to the Greek way of thinking. Instead, the Divine Law was replaced by something called the "Moral Law." The Moral Law, which was

157

said to spring from human reason rather than from God, was a system of rules specifying which actions are right. Our duty as moral persons, it was said, is to follow those rules. Thus, modern moral philosophers approached their subject by asking a question fundamentally different from the one asked by the ancients. Instead of asking *What traits of character make someone a good person?* they asked *What is the right thing to do?* This led them in a different direction. They went on to develop theories, not of virtue, but of rightness and obligation:

- *Ethical Egoism:* Each person ought to do whatever will best promote his or her own interests.
- *The Social Contract Theory:* The right thing to do is to follow the rules that rational, self-interested people would agree to follow for their mutual benefit.
- *Utilitarianism:* One ought to do whatever will lead to the most happiness.
- *Kant's theory:* Our duty is to follow rules that we could accept as universal laws—that is, rules that we would be willing for everyone to follow in all circumstances.

And these are the theories that have dominated moral philosophy from the 17th century on.

Should We Return to Virtue Ethics?   Recently, however, a number of philosophers have advanced a radical idea. Moral philosophy, they say, is bankrupt, and we should return to Aristotle's way of thinking.

This was suggested by Elizabeth Anscombe in her article "Modern Moral Philosophy" (1958). Anscombe believes that modern moral philosophy is misguided because it rests on the incoherent notion of a "law" without a lawgiver. The very concepts of obligation, duty, and rightness, she says, are inseparable from this self-contradictory notion. Therefore, we should stop thinking about obligation, duty, and rightness, and return to Aristotle's approach. The virtues should once again take center stage.

In the wake of Anscombe's article, a flood of books and essays appeared discussing the virtues, and Virtue Ethics soon became a major option again. In what follows, we will first take a look at what Virtue Ethics is like. Then we will consider some reasons for preferring this theory to other, more modern ways of approaching the subject. Finally, we will consider whether a return to Virtue Ethics would be desirable.

12.2. The Virtues

A theory of virtue should have several components: a statement of what a virtue is, a list of the virtues, an account of what these virtues consist in, and an explanation of why these qualities are good. In addition, the theory should tell us whether the virtues are the same for all people or whether they differ from person to person or from culture to culture.

What Is a Virtue? Aristotle said that a virtue is a trait of character manifested in habitual action. The word "habitual" here is important. The virtue of honesty, for example, is not possessed by someone who tells the truth only occasionally or only when it benefits her. The honest person is truthful as a matter of course; her actions "spring from a firm and unchangeable character."

But this does not distinguish virtues from vices, for vices are also traits of character manifested in habitual action. The other part of the definition is evaluative: virtues are good, whereas vices are bad. Thus, a virtue is a *commendable* trait of character manifested in habitual action. Saying this, of course, doesn't tell us which traits of character are good or bad. Later we will flesh this out by discussing the ways in which some particular virtues are good. For now, we may note that virtuous qualities are those qualities that will make us seek out someone's company. As Edmund L. Pincoffs (1919–1991) put it, "Some sorts of persons we prefer; others we avoid. The properties on our list [of virtues and vices] can serve as reasons for preference or avoidance."

We seek out people for different purposes, and this affects which virtues are relevant. In looking for an auto mechanic, we want someone who is skillful, honest, and conscientious; in looking for a teacher, we want someone who is knowledgeable, articulate, and patient. Thus, the virtues of auto repair are different from the virtues of teaching. But we also assess people *as people,* in a more general way, so we also have the concept of a good person. The moral virtues are the virtues of persons as such. Thus, we may define a moral virtue as *a trait of character, manifested in habitual action, that it is good for anyone to have.*

What Are the Virtues? What, then, are the virtues? Which traits of character should be fostered in human beings? There is no short answer, but the following is a partial list:

benevolence	fairness	patience
civility	friendliness	prudence
compassion	generosity	reasonableness
conscientiousness	honesty	self-discipline
cooperativeness	industriousness	self-reliance
courage	justice	tactfulness
courteousness	loyalty	thoughtfulness
dependability	moderation	tolerance

This list could be expanded, of course.

What Do These Virtues Consist In? It is one thing to say, in general, that we should be conscientious, compassionate, and tolerant; it is another thing to say exactly what these character traits are. Each of the virtues has its own distinctive features and raises its own distinctive problems. Let's consider four examples.

 1. *Courage.* According to Aristotle, virtues are midpoints between extremes: A virtue is "the mean by reference to two vices: the one of excess and the other of deficiency." Courage is a mean between the extremes of cowardice and foolhardiness—it is cowardly to run away from all danger, yet it is foolhardy to risk too much.

 Courage is sometimes said to be a military virtue because soldiers so obviously need to have it. But soldiers are not the only ones who need courage. We all need courage, and not just when we face a preexisting danger, such as an enemy soldier or a grizzly bear. Sometimes we need the courage to *create* a situation that will be unpleasant for us. It takes courage to apologize. If a friend is grieving, it takes courage to ask her directly how she is doing. It takes courage to volunteer to do something nice that you don't really want to do.

 If we consider only ordinary cases, the nature of courage seems unproblematic. But unusual circumstances present more troublesome cases. Consider the 19 hijackers who murdered almost 3,000 people on September 11, 2001. They faced certain death, evidently without flinching, but in the service of an evil cause. Were they courageous? The American political commentator Bill Maher implied that they were—and so he lost his television show, *Politically Incorrect*. But was Maher correct? The philosopher Peter Geach wouldn't think so. "Courage in an unworthy cause," he says, "is no virtue; still less is courage in an evil cause. Indeed I prefer not to call this nonvirtuous facing of danger 'courage.'"

It is easy to see Geach's point. Calling a terrorist "courageous" seems to praise his performance, and we do not want to do that. But, on the other hand, it doesn't seem quite right to say that he is *not* courageous—after all, look at how he behaves in the face of danger. To resolve this dilemma, perhaps we should just say that he displays two qualities of character, one admirable (steadfastness in facing danger) and one detestable (a willingness to kill innocent people). He is courageous, as Maher suggested, and courage is a good thing; but because his courage is deployed in such an evil cause, his behavior is *on the whole* extremely wicked.

2. *Generosity.* Generosity is the willingness to give to others. One can be generous with any of one's resources—with one's time, for example, or one's money or one's knowledge. Aristotle says that generosity, like courage, is a mean between extremes: It falls between stinginess and extravagance. The stingy person gives too little; the extravagant person gives too much; the generous person gives just the right amount. But what amount is just right?

Another ancient teacher, Jesus of Nazareth, said that we must give everything we have to the poor. Jesus considered it wrong to possess riches while other people are dying of starvation. Those who heard Jesus speak found his teaching too demanding, and they generally rejected it. Human nature has not changed much in the last 2,000 years: today, few people follow Jesus's advice, even among those who claim to admire him.

On this issue, the modern utilitarians are Jesus's moral descendants. They hold that in every circumstance it is our duty to do whatever will have the best overall consequences for everyone concerned. This means that we should be generous with our money until further giving would harm us as much as it would help others. In other words, we should give until we ourselves become the most worthy recipients of whatever money remains in our hands. If we did this, then we would become poor.

Why do people resist this idea? The main reason may be self-interest; we do not want to become destitute. But this is about more than money; it is also about time and energy. Adopting such a policy would prevent us from living normal lives. Our lives consist of projects and relationships that require a considerable investment of money, time, and effort. An ideal of "generosity" that demands too much of us would require us to abandon our everyday lives. We'd have to live like saints.

A reasonable interpretation of generosity might therefore be something like this: We should be as generous with our resources as we can be while still carrying on our normal lives. But even this interpretation leaves us with an awkward question. Some people's "normal lives" are quite extravagant—think of a rich person who has grown accustomed to great luxuries. Surely such a person can't be generous unless he is willing to sell his yacht to feed the hungry. The virtue of generosity, it would seem, cannot exist in the context of a life that is too opulent. So, to make this interpretation of generosity "reasonable," our conception of normal life must not be too extravagant.

3. *Honesty.* The honest person is someone who, first of all, does not lie. But is that enough? Lying is not the only way of misleading people. Geach tells the story of Saint Athanasius, who "was rowing on a river when the persecutors came rowing in the opposite direction: 'Where is the traitor Athanasius?' 'Not far away,' the Saint gaily replied, and rowed past them unsuspected."

Geach approves of the saint's deception, even though he would disapprove of the saint's telling an outright lie. Lying, according to Geach, is always forbidden: someone possessing the virtue of honesty will never even consider it. Honest people do not lie; so, they must find other ways of attaining their goals. Athanasius found such a way, even in his predicament. He did not lie to his pursuers; he "merely" deceived them. But isn't deception dishonest? Why should some ways of misleading people be dishonest, and others not?

To answer that question, let's think about why honesty is a virtue to begin with. Why is honesty good? Part of the reason is large-scale: Civilization depends on it. Our ability to live together in communities depends on our ability to communicate. We talk to one another, read each other's writing, exchange information and opinions, express our desires to one another, make promises, ask and answer questions, and much more. Without these sorts of exchanges, social living would be impossible. But people must be honest for such exchanges to work.

On a smaller scale, when we take people at their word, we make ourselves vulnerable to them. By accepting what they say and modifying our behavior accordingly, we place our well-being in their hands. If they speak truthfully, all is well. But if they lie, then we end up with false beliefs; and if we act on those beliefs, then we do foolish things. We trusted them, and they betrayed our trust. Dishonesty is manipulative. By contrast, honest people treat others with respect.

If these ideas account for why honesty is a virtue, then lies and "deceptive truths" are both dishonest. After all, both types of deceit are objectionable for the same reasons. Both have the same goal: the point of lying *and* deceiving is to make the listener acquire a false belief. In Geach's example, Athanasius got his persecutors to believe that he was not in fact Athanasius. Had Athanasius lied to his pursuers, rather than merely deceiving them, then his words would have served the same purpose. Because both actions aim at false beliefs, both can disrupt the smooth functioning of society, and both violate trust. If you accuse someone of lying to you, and she responds by saying that she did not lie—she "merely" deceived you—then you would not be impressed. Either way, she took advantage of your trust and manipulated you into believing something false. The honest person will neither lie nor deceive.

But will the honest person *never* lie? Geach's example raises the question of whether virtue requires adherence to absolute rules. Let's distinguish two views:

1. An honest person will never lie or deceive.
2. An honest person will never lie or deceive except in rare circumstances when there are compelling reasons to do so.

Despite Geach's protest, there are good reasons to favor the second view, even with regard to lying.

First, remember that honesty is not the only thing we value. In a specific situation, some other value might get priority—for example, the value of self-preservation. Suppose Saint Athanasius had lied and said, "I don't know where that traitor is," and as a result, his pursuers went off on a wild-goose chase. Now the saint would get to live another day. If this had occurred, most of us would continue to regard Saint Athanasius as honest. We would merely say that he valued his own life more than the telling of one lie.

Moreover, if we consider why honesty is good, then we can see that Athanasius would have been justified in lying to his pursuers. Obviously, that particular lie would not have disrupted the smooth functioning of society. But wouldn't it at least have violated the trust of the people who were pursuing him? The response is that, if lying is a violation of trust, then for lying to be immoral, the person you're lying to must *deserve* your trust. But in this case, the saint's pursuers did not deserve his trust, because they were persecuting him unjustly. Thus, even an honest person may sometimes lie or deceive with full justification.

4. *Loyalty to friends and family.* Friendship is essential to the good life. As Aristotle says, "No one would choose to live without friends, even if he had all other goods":

> How could prosperity be safeguarded and preserved without friends? The greater our prosperity is, the greater are the risks it brings with it. Also, in poverty and all other kinds of misfortune men believe that their only refuge consists in their friends. Friends help young men avoid error; to older people they give the care and help needed to supplement the failing powers of action which infirmity brings.

The benefits of friendship, of course, go far beyond material assistance. Psychologically, we would be lost without our friends. Our triumphs seem hollow without friends to share them with, and we need our friends even more when we fail. Our self-esteem depends in large measure on the assurances of friends: By returning our affection, they confirm our worth as human beings.

If we need friends, then we need the qualities that enable us to *be* a friend. Near the top of the list is loyalty. Friends can be counted on. You stick by your friends even when things are going badly and even when, objectively speaking, you should abandon them. Friends make allowances for one another; they forgive offenses and refrain from harsh judgments. There are limits, of course—sometimes only a friend can tell us the hard truth about ourselves. But criticism is acceptable from friends because we know that they are not rejecting us.

None of this is to deny that we have duties to other people, even to strangers. But those duties are associated with different virtues. Generalized beneficence is a virtue, and it may demand a great deal, but it does not require the same level of concern for strangers as for friends. Justice is another such virtue; it requires impartial treatment for all. But friends are loyal to one another, so the demands of justice are weaker when friends are involved.

We are even closer to family members than we are to friends, so we may show family members even more loyalty and partiality. In Plato's *Euthyphro,* Socrates learns that Euthyphro has come to the courthouse to prosecute his own father for murder. Socrates expresses surprise at this and wonders whether a son should bring charges against his father. Euthyphro sees no impropriety: For him, a murder is a murder. Euthyphro has a point, but we might still be shocked that someone could take the same attitude toward his father that he would take toward a stranger. A close family member, we might think, need not be involved in such a legal matter. This point is recognized in American law: In the United States, one cannot be compelled to testify in court against one's husband or wife.

Why Are the Virtues Important? We said that virtues are traits of character that are good for people to have. This raises the question of why the virtues are good. Why should a person be courageous, generous, honest, or loyal? The answer may depend on the virtue in question. Thus:

- Courage is good because we need it to cope with danger.
- Generosity is desirable because there will always be people who need help.
- Honesty is needed because without it relations between people would go wrong in all sorts of ways.
- Loyalty is essential to friendship; friends stand by one another even when others would turn away.

This list suggests that each virtue is valuable for a different reason. However, Aristotle offers a general answer to our question—he says that the virtues are important because the virtuous person will fare better in life. The point is not that the virtuous will always be richer; the point is that we need the virtues in order to flourish.

To see what Aristotle is getting at, consider who we are and how we live. On the most general level, we are social creatures who want the company of others. So we live in communities among family, friends, and fellow citizens. In this setting, such qualities as loyalty, fairness, and honesty are needed to interact success-fully with others. On a more individual level, we might have a job and pursue particular interests. Those endeavors might call for other virtues, such as perseverance and industriousness. Finally, it is part of our common human condition that we must some-times face danger or temptation, so courage and self-control are needed. Thus, the virtues all have the same general sort of value: They are all qualities needed for successful living.

Are the Virtues the Same for Everyone? Finally, we may ask whether a single set of traits is desirable for all people. Should we speak of *the* good person, as though all good people come from one mold? Friedrich Nietzsche (1844–1900) thought not. In his flamboyant way, Nietzsche observes:

> How naive it is altogether to say: "Man *ought* to be such-and-such!" Reality shows us an enchanting wealth of types, the abundance of a lavish play and change of forms—and some wretched loafer of a moralist comments: "No! Man ought to be different." He even knows what man should be like, this wretched bigot and prig: he paints himself on the wall and comments, *"Ecce homo!"* ["Behold the man!"]

There is obviously something to this. The scholar who devotes his life to understanding medieval literature and the profes-sional soldier are very different kinds of people. A Victorian woman who would never expose a leg in public and a woman who sunbathes on a nude beach have very different standards of modesty. And yet all may be admirable in their own ways.

There is, then, an obvious sense in which the virtues may differ from person to person. Because people lead different kinds of lives, have different sorts of personalities, and occupy different social roles, the qualities of character that help them flourish may differ.

It is tempting to go even further and say that the virtues differ from society to society. After all, the kind of life that is pos-sible will depend on the values and institutions that dominate a region. A scholar's life is possible only where there are institu-tions, such as universities, that make intellectual investigation possible. Much the same could be said about being an athlete, a priest, a geisha, or a samurai warrior. The character traits that are needed to occupy those roles will differ, and so the traits needed to live successfully will differ. Thus, the virtues will be different.

To this, it may be answered that *certain virtues will be needed by all people in all times.* This was Aristotle's view, and he was probably right. Aristotle believed that we all have a great deal in common, despite our differences. "One may observe," he says, "in one's travels to distant countries the feelings of recognition and affiliation that link every human being to every other human being." Even in the most disparate societies, people face the same basic problems and have the same basic needs. Thus:

- Everyone needs courage, because no one (not even the scholar) can always avoid danger. Also, everyone needs the courage to take the occasional risk.
- In every society, there will be some people who are worse off than others; so, generosity will always be prized.
- Honesty is always a virtue because no society can exist without dependable communication.
- Everyone needs friends, and to have friends one must be a friend; so, everyone needs loyalty.

This sort of list could—and in Aristotle's hands it does—go on and on.

To summarize, then, it may be true that in different societies the virtues are given different interpretations, and different actions may be counted as satisfying them; and it may be true that the value of a character trait will vary from person to person and from society to society. But it cannot be right to say that social customs determine whether any particular character trait is a virtue. The major virtues flow from our common human condition.

12.3. Two Advantages of Virtue Ethics

Virtue Ethics is often said to have two selling points.

1. *Moral motivation.* Virtue Ethics is appealing because it provides a natural and attractive account of moral motivation. Consider the following:

You are in the hospital recovering from a long illness. You are bored and restless, and so you are delighted when Smith comes to visit. You have a good time talking to him; his visit really cheers you up. After a while, you tell Smith how much you enjoy seeing him—he really is a good friend to take the trouble to come see you. But, Smith says, he is merely doing his duty. At first you think he is only being modest, but the more you talk, the clearer it becomes that he is speaking the literal truth. He is not visiting you because he wants to or because he likes you, but only because he thinks he should "do the right thing." He feels it is his duty to visit you, perhaps because you are worse off than anyone else he knows.

This example was suggested by the American philosopher Michael Stocker (1940–). As Stocker points out, you'd be very disappointed to learn Smith's motive; now his visit seems cold and calculating. You thought he was your friend, but now you know otherwise. Commenting on Smith's behavior, Stocker says, "Surely there is something lacking here—and lacking in moral merit or value."

Of course, there is nothing wrong with *what* Smith did. The problem is *why* he did it. We value friendship, love, and respect, and we want our relationships to be based on mutual regard. Acting from an abstract sense of duty or from a desire to "do the right thing" is not the same. We would not want to live in a community of people who acted only from such motives, nor would we want to be such a person ourselves. Therefore, the argument goes, theories that focus on right action cannot provide a completely satisfactory account of the moral life. For that, we need a theory that emphasizes personal qualities such as friendship, love, and loyalty—in other words, a theory of the virtues.

2. *Doubts about the "ideal" of impartiality.* A dominant theme in modern moral philosophy has been impartiality—the idea that all persons are morally equal, and that we should treat everyone's interests as equally important. The utilitarian theory is typical. "Utilitarianism," John Stuart Mill writes, "requires [the moral agent] to be as strictly impartial as a disinterested and benevolent spectator." The book you are now reading also treats impartiality as a fundamental ethical requirement: In the first chapter, impartiality was included in the "minimum conception" of morality.

It may be doubted, though, whether impartiality is really such a noble ideal. Consider our relationships with family and friends. Should we be impartial where their interests are concerned? A mother loves her children and cares for them in a way that she does not care for other children. She is partial to them through and through. But is anything wrong with that? Isn't that exactly the way a mother should be? Again, we love our friends, and we are willing to do things for them that we would not do for others. What's wrong with that? Loving relationships are essential to the good life. But any theory that emphasizes impartiality will have a hard time accounting for this.

A moral theory that emphasizes the virtues, however, can easily account for all this. Some virtues are partial and some are not. Loyalty involves partiality toward loved ones and friends; beneficence involves equal regard for everyone. What is needed is not some general requirement of impartiality, but an understanding of how these virtues relate to one another.

12.4. Virtue and Conduct

As we have seen, theories that emphasize right action seem incomplete because they neglect the question of character. Virtue Ethics remedies this problem by making character its central concern. But as a result, Virtue Ethics runs the risk of being incomplete in the other direction. Moral problems are frequently problems about what to *do*. What can a theory of virtue tell us about the assessment, not of character, but of action?

The answer will depend on the spirit in which Virtue Ethics is offered. On the one hand, we might combine the best features of the right-action approach with insights drawn from the virtues approach—we might try to improve Utilitarianism or Kantianism, for example, by supplementing them with a theory of moral character. This seems sensible. If so, then we can assess right action simply by relying on Utilitarianism or Kantianism.

On the other hand, some writers believe that Virtue Ethics should be understood as an *alternative* to the other theories. These writers believe that Virtue Ethics is a complete moral theory in itself. We might call this *Radical Virtue Ethics*. What would such a theory say about right action? Either it will need to dispense with the notion of "right action" altogether, or it will have to give some account of the idea derived from the conception of virtuous character.

It might sound crazy, but some philosophers have argued that we should get rid of such concepts as "morally right action." Anscombe says that "it would be a great improvement" if we stopped using such notions. We could still assess conduct as better or worse, she says, but we would do so in other terms. Instead of saying that an action was "morally wrong," we would say that it was "intolerant" or "unjust" or "cowardly"—terms derived from the vocabulary of virtue. On her view, such terms allow us to say everything that we need to say.

But advocates of Radical Virtue Ethics need not reject notions such as "morally right." These ideas can be retained but given a new interpretation within the virtue framework. We could still assess actions based on the reasons that can be given for or against them. However, *the reasons cited will all be reasons connected with the virtues.* Thus, the reasons for doing some particular action might be that it is honest, or generous, or fair; while the reasons against doing it might be that it is dishonest, or stingy, or unfair. On this approach, the right thing to do is whatever a virtuous person would do.

12.5. The Problem of Incompleteness

The main objection to Radical Virtue Ethics is that it is incomplete. It seems to be incomplete in three ways.

First, Radical Virtue Ethics cannot explain everything it should explain. Consider a typical virtue, such as dependability. Why should I be dependable? Plainly, we need an answer to this question that goes beyond the simple observation that being dependable is a virtue. We want to know *why* dependability is a virtue; we want to know why it is good. Possible explanations might be that being dependable is to one's own advantage, or being dependable promotes the general welfare, or dependability is needed by those who must live together and rely on one another. The first explanation looks suspiciously like Ethical Egoism; the second is utilitarian; and the third recalls the Social Contract Theory. But none of these explanations are couched in terms of the virtues. Any explanation of why a particular virtue is good, it seems, would have to take us beyond the narrow confines of Radical Virtue Ethics.

If Radical Virtue Ethics doesn't explain *why* something is a virtue, then it won't be able to tell us whether the virtues apply in difficult cases. Consider the virtue of being beneficent, or being kind. Suppose I hear some news that would upset you to know about. Maybe I've learned that someone you used to know died in a car accident. If I don't tell you this, you might never find out. Suppose, also, that you're the sort of person who would want to be told. If I know all this, should I tell you the news? What would be the *kind* thing to do? It's a hard question, because what you would prefer—being told—conflicts with what would make you feel good—not being told. Would a kind person care more about what you want, or more about what makes you feel good? Radical Virtue Ethics cannot answer this question. To be kind is to look out for someone's best interests; but Radical Virtue Ethics does not tell us what someone's best interests are. So, the second way in which the theory is incomplete is that it cannot give a full interpretation of the virtues. It cannot say exactly when they apply.

Finally, Radical Virtue Ethics is incomplete because it cannot help us deal with cases of moral conflict. Suppose I just got a haircut—a mullet the likes of which have not been seen since 1992—and I put you on the spot by asking you what you think. You can either tell me the truth, or you can say I look just fine. Honesty and kindness are both virtues, and so there are reasons both for and against each alternative. But you must do one or the other—you must either tell the truth and be unkind, or not tell the truth and be kind. Which should you do? If someone told you, "Well, you should act virtuously in this situation," that wouldn't help you decide what to do; it would only leave you wondering which virtue to follow. Clearly, we need guidance beyond the resources of Radical Virtue Ethics.

By itself, it seems, Radical Virtue Ethics is limited to platitudes: be kind, be honest, be patient, be generous, and so on. Platitudes are vague, and when they conflict, we must look beyond them for guidance. Radical Virtue Ethics needs the resources of a larger theory.

12.6. Conclusion

It seems best to regard Virtue Ethics as part of our overall theory of ethics rather than as being a complete theory in itself. The total theory would include an account of all the considerations that figure in practical decision making, together with their underlying rationales. The question is whether such a theory can accommodate both an adequate conception of right action and a related conception of virtuous character.

I don't see why not. Suppose, for example, that we accept a utilitarian theory of right action—we believe that one ought to do whatever will lead to the most happiness. From a moral point of view, we would want a society in which everyone leads happy and satisfying lives. We could then ask which actions, which social policies, *and which qualities of character* would most likely lead to that result. An inquiry into the nature of virtue could then be conducted from within that larger framework.

CHAPTER 13

What Would a Satisfactory Moral Theory Be Like?

> Some people believe that there cannot be progress in
> Ethics, since everything has already been said. . . . I believe
> the opposite. . . . Compared with the other sciences,
> Non-Religious Ethics is the youngest and least advanced.
> DEREK PARFIT, *REASONS AND PERSONS* (1984)

13.1. Morality without Hubris

Moral philosophy has a rich and fascinating history. Scholars have approached the subject from many different perspectives, producing theories that both attract and repel the thoughtful reader. Almost all the classical theories contain plausible elements, which is hardly surprising, since they were devised by philosophers of undoubted genius. Yet the various theories conflict with each other, and most of them are vulnerable to crippling objections. One is left wondering what to believe. What, in the final analysis, is the truth? Of course, different philosophers would answer this question in different ways. Some might refuse to give an answer, on the grounds that we do not know enough to have reached the "final analysis." In this respect, moral philosophy is not much worse off than any other subject—we do not know the final truth about most things. But we do know a lot, and it might not be rash to say something about what a satisfactory moral theory might be like.

A Modest Conception of Human Beings. A satisfactory theory would be realistic about where human beings fit in the grand scheme of things. The "big bang" occurred some 13.7 billion years ago, and the earth was formed around 4.5 billion years

173

ago. Life on earth evolved slowly, mostly according to the principles of natural selection. When the dinosaurs went extinct 65 million years ago, this left more room for the evolution of mammals, and a few hundred thousand years ago, one line of that evolution produced us. In geological time, we arrived only yesterday.

But no sooner did our ancestors arrive than they began to think of themselves as the crown of creation. Some of them even imagined that the whole universe had been made for their benefit. Thus, when they began to develop theories of right and wrong, they held that the protection of their own interests had a kind of ultimate and objective value. The rest of creation, they reasoned, was intended for their use. But now we know better. We now know that we exist by evolutionary accident, as one species among millions, on one small speck of an unimaginably vast cosmos. The details of this picture are revised each year, as more is discovered, but the main outlines are well established. Some of the old story remains: human beings are still the smartest animals we know and the only ones that use language. Those facts, however, cannot justify an entire worldview that places us at the center.

How Reason Gives Rise to Ethics.   Human beings have evolved as rational beings. Because we are rational, we are able to take some facts as reasons for behaving one way rather than another. We can articulate those reasons and think about them. Thus, if an action would help satisfy our desires, needs, and so on—in short, if it would *promote our interests*—then we take that as a reason to do it.

The origin of our concept of "ought" may be found in these facts. If we were incapable of considering reasons, we would have no use for such a notion. Like the other animals, we would act from instinct or habit. But the examination of reasons introduces a new factor. Now we find ourselves driven to act in certain ways as a result of deliberation—as a result of thinking about our behavior and its consequences. We use the word *ought* to mark this new element of the situation: We ought to do what there are the strongest reasons for doing.

Once we see morality as a matter of acting on reason, another important point emerges. In reasoning about what to do, we can be consistent or inconsistent. One way of being inconsistent is to accept a fact as a reason on one occasion but to reject it as a reason on a similar occasion. This happens when one places the interests of one's own race above the interests of other races, despite the absence of any reason to do so. Racism is an offense against morality because it is an offense against reason. Similar remarks apply to other doctrines that divide humanity into the morally favored and disfavored, such as nationalism, sexism, and classism. The upshot is that reason requires impartiality: We ought to act so as to promote the interests of everyone alike.

If Psychological Egoism were true—if we could care only about ourselves—this would mean that reason demands more of us than we can manage. But Psychological Egoism is not true; it presents a false picture of human nature and the human condition. We have evolved as social creatures, living together in groups, wanting one another's company, needing one another's cooperation, and capable of caring about one another's welfare. So there is a pleasing "fit" between (a) what reason requires, namely, impartiality; (b) the requirements of social living, namely, adherence to rules that serve everyone's interests, if fairly applied; and (c) our natural inclination to care about others, at least to a modest degree. All three work together to make morality not only possible but *natural* for us.

13.2. Treating People as They Deserve

The idea that we should "promote the interests of everyone alike" is appealing when it is used to refute bigotry. However, sometimes there is good reason to treat people differently— sometimes people *deserve* to be treated better or worse than others. Human beings are rational agents who can make free choices. Those who choose to treat others well deserve good treatment; those who choose to treat others badly deserve ill treatment.

This sounds harsh until we consider examples. Suppose Smith has always been generous, helping you whenever she could, and now she is in trouble and needs your help. You now have a special reason to help her, beyond the general obligation you have to be helpful to everyone. She is not just a member of the great crowd of humanity; she has earned your respect and gratitude through her conduct.

By contrast, consider someone with the opposite history. Your neighbor Jones has always refused to help you out. One day, for example, your car wouldn't start, and he wouldn't give you a ride to work—he just couldn't be bothered. Some time later, though, *he* has car trouble and asks *you* for a ride. Now Jones deserves to have to fend for himself. If you gave him a ride despite his past behavior, you would be choosing to treat him better than he deserves.

Treating people as they have chosen to treat others is not just a matter of rewarding friends and holding grudges against enemies. It is a matter of treating people as responsible agents who merit particular responses, based on their past conduct. There is an important difference between Smith and Jones: one of them deserves our gratitude; the other deserves our resentment. What would it be like if we did not care about such things?

For one thing, we would be denying people the ability to earn good treatment at the hands of others. This is important. Because we live in communities, how each of us fares depends not only on what we do but on what others do as well. If we are to flourish, we need others to treat us well. A social system in which deserts are acknowledged gives us a way of doing that; it is a way of granting people the power to determine their own fates.

Absent this, what are we to do? We might imagine a system in which a person can get good treatment only by force, or by luck, or as a matter of charity. But the practice of acknowledging deserts is different. It gives people control over whether others will treat them well or badly. It says to them, "If you behave well, you will be *entitled* to good treatment from others. You will have earned it." Acknowledging deserts is ultimately about treating other people with respect.

13.3. A Variety of Motives

There are other ways in which the idea of "promoting the interests of everyone alike" apparently fails to capture the whole of moral life. (I say "apparently" because I will ask later whether it really does.) Certainly, people should sometimes be motivated by an impartial concern for others. But there are other morally praiseworthy motives:

- A mother loves and cares for her children. She does not want to "promote their interests" simply because they are people she can help. Her attitude toward them is entirely different from her attitude toward other children. While she might want to help other children when she can, that vaguely benevolent feeling is nothing like the love she has for her own.
- A man is loyal to his friends. Again, he is not concerned with their interests only as part of his concern for people generally. They are his friends, and so they are special to him.

Only a philosophical fool would want to eliminate love, loyalty, and the like from our understanding of the moral life. If such motives were eliminated, and instead people simply calculated what was best, we would all be much worse off. Anyway, who would want to live in a world without love and friendship?

Of course, people may have many other valuable motives:

- A composer is concerned, above all else, to finish her symphony. She pursues this even though she might do "more good" by doing something else.
- A teacher devotes great effort to preparing his classes, even though more good might be done by directing his energy elsewhere.

While these motives are not usually considered "moral," we should not want to eliminate them from human life. Taking pride in one's job, wanting to create something of value, and many other noble intentions contribute to both personal happiness and the general welfare. We should no more want to eliminate them than to eliminate love and friendship.

13.4. Multiple-Strategies Utilitarianism

Above, I gave a sketchy justification of the principle that "we ought to act so as to promote the interests of everyone alike." But then I noted that this cannot be the whole story about our moral obligations because sometimes we should treat people differently, according to their individual deserts. And then I discussed some morally important motives that seem unrelated to the impartial promotion of interests.

Yet it may be possible to see these diverse concerns as interrelated. At first blush, it seems that treating people according to their individual deserts is quite different from seeking to promote the interests of everyone alike. But when we asked why deserts are important, the answer turned out to be that *we would all be much worse off* if acknowledging deserts was not part of our social scheme. And when we ask why love, friendship, artistic creativity, and pride in one's work are important, the answer is that *our lives would be so much poorer* without such things. This suggests that there is a single standard at work in our assessments.

Perhaps, then, the single moral standard is human welfare. What is important is that people be as happy as possible. This standard can be used to assess a wide variety of things, including actions, policies, social customs, laws, rules, motives, and character traits. But this does not mean that we should always think in terms of making people as happy as possible. Our day-to-day lives will go better if, instead, we simply love our children, enjoy our friends, take pride in our work, keep our promises, and so on. An ethic that values "the interests of everyone alike" will endorse this conclusion.

This is not a new idea. Henry Sidgwick (1838–1900), the great utilitarian theorist of the Victorian era, made the same point:

> The doctrine that Universal Happiness is the ultimate *standard* must not be understood to imply that Universal Benevolence is the only right or always best *motive* of action . . . it is not necessary that the end which gives the criterion of rightness should always be the end at which we consciously aim: and if experience shows that the general happiness will be more satisfactorily attained if men frequently act from other motives than pure universal philanthropy, it is obvious that these other motives are reasonably to be preferred on Utilitarian principles.

This passage has been cited in support of a view called "Motive Utilitarianism." According to that view, we should act from the motives that best promote the general welfare.

Yet the most plausible view of this type does not focus exclusively on motives; nor does it focus entirely on acts or rules, as other theories have done. The most plausible theory might be called *Multiple-Strategies Utilitarianism*. This theory is utilitarian, because the ultimate goal is to maximize the general welfare.

However, the theory recognizes that we may use diverse strategies to pursue that goal. Sometimes we aim directly at it. For example, a senator may support a bill because she believes that it would raise the standard of living for everyone, or an individual may send money to the International Red Cross because he believes that this would do more good than any other action he might perform. But usually we don't think of the general welfare at all; instead, we simply care for our children, work at our jobs, obey the law, keep our promises, and so on.

Right Action as Living According to the Best Plan. We can make the idea behind Multiple-Strategies Utilitarianism a little more specific.

Suppose we had a fully specified list of the virtues, motives, and methods of decision making that would enable a person to be happy and to contribute to the welfare of others. And suppose, further, that this is the *optimum* list for that person; there is no other combination of virtues, motives, and methods of decision making that would do a better job. The list would include at least the following:

- The virtues that are needed to make one's life go well
- The motives on which to act
- The commitments that one will have to friends, family, and others
- The social roles that one will occupy, with the responsibilities and demands that go with them
- The duties and concerns associated with the projects one will undertake, such as becoming a DJ or a soldier or an undertaker
- The everyday rules that one will usually follow without even thinking
- A strategy, or group of strategies, about when to consider making exceptions to the rules, and the grounds on which those exceptions can be made

The list would also specify the relations between the different items on the list—what takes priority over what, how to adjudicate conflicts, and so on. It would be very hard to construct such a list. As a practical matter, it might even be impossible. But we can be fairly sure that it would include endorsements of friendship, honesty, and other familiar virtues. It would tell us to keep our promises, but not always, and to refrain from harming people, but not always; and so on. And it would probably tell us to stop living in luxury while millions of children die of preventable diseases.

At any rate, there is some combination of virtues, motives, and methods of decision making that is best *for me,* given my circumstances, personality, and talents—"best" in the sense that it will optimize the chances of my having a good life, while optimizing the chances of other people having good lives, too. Call this optimum combination *my best plan.* The right thing for me to do is to act in accordance with my best plan.

My best plan may have a lot in common with yours. Presumably, they will both include rules against lying, stealing, and killing, together with an understanding about when to make exceptions to those rules. They will both include virtues such as patience, kindness, and self-control. They may both contain instructions for raising children, including what virtues to foster in them.

But our best plans need not be identical. People have different personalities and talents. One person may find fulfillment as a priest while another could never live like that. Thus, our lives might include different sorts of personal relationships, and we might need to cultivate different virtues. People also live in different circumstances and have access to different resources—some are rich; some are poor; some are privileged; some are persecuted. Thus, the optimum strategies for living will differ.

In each case, however, the identification of a plan as the best plan will be a matter of assessing how well it promotes the interests of everyone alike. So the overall theory is utilitarian, even though it may frequently endorse motives that do not look utilitarian at all.

13.5. The Moral Community

As moral agents, we should be concerned with everyone whose welfare might be affected by what we do. This may seem like a pious platitude, but in reality it can be a hard doctrine. Around the world, one child in five fails to get essential vaccinations, resulting in about two million unnecessary deaths each year. Citizens in the affluent countries could easily cut this number in half, but they won't. People would no doubt do more if children in their own neighborhoods were dying, but the location of the children shouldn't matter: Everyone is included in the community of moral concern. If the interests of all children, no matter where they lived, were taken seriously, it would force us to change our ways.

If the moral community is not limited to people in one *place*, neither is it limited to people at any one *time*. Whether people will be affected by our actions now or in the future is irrelevant. Our obligation is to consider all their interests equally. One consequence of this pertains to nuclear weapons. Such weapons not only have the power to maim and kill innocent people, but they can also poison the environment for thousands of years. If the welfare of future generations is given proper weight, it is difficult to imagine any circumstance in which such weapons should be used. Climate change is another issue that affects the interests of our descendants. If we fail to reverse the effects of global warming, our children will suffer even more than we will.

There is one other way in which our conception of the moral community must be expanded. Humans are not alone on this planet. Other sentient animals—that is, animals capable of feeling pleasure and pain—also have interests. When we abuse them or kill them, they are harmed, just as humans can be harmed in those ways. Bentham and Mill were right to insist that the interests of nonhuman animals must be included in our moral calculations. As Bentham pointed out, excluding creatures from moral consideration because of their species is no more justified than excluding them because of their race, nationality, or sex. So, the single moral standard is not human welfare, but sentient welfare.

13.6. Justice and Fairness

Utilitarianism has been criticized as unfair and unjust. Can the complications we have introduced help?

One criticism concerns punishment. We can imagine cases in which it would promote the general welfare to frame an innocent person. Such an act would be blatantly unjust, yet Utilitarianism would seem to require it. More generally, as Kant pointed out, utilitarians are happy to "use" criminals for the achievement of society's ends. Even if those ends are worthwhile—such as the reduction of future crime—we might be uncomfortable with a theory that endorsed manipulation as a legitimate moral strategy.

However, our theory takes a different view of punishment than utilitarians have usually taken. In fact, our view is close to Kant's. In punishing someone, we are treating him worse than we treat others. But this is justified by the person's own past deeds: It is a response to what he has done. That is why it is not right to frame an innocent person; the innocent person has done nothing to deserve such treatment.

The theory of punishment, however, is only one aspect of justice. Questions of justice arise any time one person is treated differently from another. Suppose an employer must choose which of two employees to promote. The first candidate has worked hard, taking on extra work, giving up vacation time, and so on. The second candidate, on the other hand, has never done more than he had to. Obviously, the two employees will be treated very differently: One will get the promotion; the other will not. But this is all right, according to our theory. The first employee has earned the promotion; the second has not.

A person's voluntary actions can justify a departure from the policy of "equal treatment," but nothing else can. This goes against a common view of the matter. Often, people think it is right for individuals to be rewarded for physical beauty, superior intelligence, and other qualities that are due, in large part, to having the right DNA and being raised by the right parents. And in practice, people often have better jobs and more money just because they were born with greater natural gifts into wealthier families. But on reflection, this does not seem right. People do not deserve their native endowments; they have them only as a result of what John Rawls (1921–2002) calls "the natural lottery." Suppose the first employee in our example was passed over for the promotion, despite her hard work, because the second employee had some natural ability that was more useful in the new position. Even if the employer could justify this decision in terms of the company's needs, the first employee would rightly feel cheated. She has worked harder, yet he is getting the promotion, and the benefits that go with it, because of something he did nothing to earn. That is not fair. In a just society, people could improve their circumstances through hard work, but they would not benefit from a lucky birth.

13.7. Conclusion

What would a satisfactory moral theory look like? I have outlined the possibility that seems most plausible to me: According to Multiple-Strategies Utilitarianism, we should maximize the interests of all sentient beings by living according to our best plan. Modesty, however, is required when making such a proposal. Over the centuries, philosophers have articulated and defended a wide variety of moral theories, and history has always found flaws in their conceptions. Still, there is hope, if not for my suggestion, then for some other proposal down the road. Civilization is only a few thousand years old. If we do not destroy it, then the study of ethics has a bright future.

Notes on Sources

Chapter 1: What Is Morality?

The ethicists' comments about Baby Theresa are from an Associated Press report by David Briggs, "Baby Theresa Case Raises Ethics Questions," *Champaign-Urbana News-Gazette*, March 31, 1992, p. A-6.

The poll about separating conjoined twins is from the *Ladies' Home Journal*, March 2001. The judges' comments about Jodie and Mary are from the *Daily Telegraph*, September 23, 2000.

Information about the Tracy Latimer case is from *The New York Times*, December 1, 1997, National Edition, p. A-3. The quotation is from the Canadian Broadcasting Corporation, January 19, 2001.

Chapter 2: The Challenge of Cultural Relativism

The story of the Greeks and the Callatians is from Herodotus, *The Histories*, translated by Aubrey de Selincourt, revised by A. R. Burn (Harmondsworth, Middlesex: Penguin Books, 1972), pp. 219–220. The quotation from Herodotus toward the end of the chapter is from the same source.

The information about the Eskimos is from Peter Freuchen, *Book of the Eskimos* (New York: Fawcett, 1961), and E. Adamson Hoebel, *The Law of Primitive Man* (Cambridge, MA: Harvard University Press, 1954), chapter 5. The estimate of how female infanticide affects the male/female ratio in the Eskimo population is from Hoebel's work.

The William Graham Sumner quotation is from his *Folkways* (Boston: Ginn, 1906), p. 28.

The New York Times series on female genital mutilation included articles (mainly by Celia W. Dugger) published in 1996 on April 15, April 25, May 2, May 3, July 8, September 11, October 5, October 12, and December 28. I also learned about Fauziya Kassindja from her interview on PBS; see http://www.pbs.org/speaktruthtopower/fauziya.html. The figures of "28 African nations" and "about 135 million" come from the World Health Organization's "An Update on WHO's Work on Female Genital Mutilation" (2011), p. 1.

The story about the Nigerian woman sentenced to death comes from Associated Press articles on August 20, 2002, and September 25, 2003. The story about the Australian woman convicted on drug charges comes from a May 27, 2005, article in *The New York Times.* The story about the Saudi woman who was sentenced to being lashed comes from *The New York Times* (articles on November 16 and December 18, 2007).

The Dan Savage quotation about monogamy is from Mark Oppenheimer, "Married, with Infidelities," *The New York Times Magazine,* July 3, 2011, pp. 22–27, 46 (quotation on p. 23).

Chapter 3: Subjectivism in Ethics

The quotation from Matt Foreman is from *The New York Times,* June 25, 2001.

The Gallup Poll information is from www.gallup.com.

"If you're involved in the gay and lesbian lifestyle, it's bondage." Michele Bachmann, speaking at *EdWatch National Education Conference,* November 6, 2004. I learned about the Bachmanns' clinic from *Anderson Cooper 360,* "Keeping Them Honest" (July 13, 2011), http://ac360.blogs.cnn.com/2011/07/13/video-ex-patient-speaks-about-clinics-therapy/.

The Catholic view about homosexuality is quoted from *Catechism of the Catholic Church* (Mahwah, NJ: Paulist Press, 1994), p. 566.

Charles L. Stevenson, *Ethics and Language* (New Haven, CT: Yale University Press, 1944). Disagreement in belief/disagreement in attitude, pp. 2–4; "*Any* statement about *any* matter of fact . . . ," p. 114.

The story about Katie Shelton and Mark Friedrich is from the Carnegie Hero Fund Commission's website: www.carnegiehero.org.

"This is a very serious matter. . . .": Michele Bachmann, on the radio program "Prophetic Views Behind the News" (hosted by Jan Markell), KKMS 980-AM, March 20, 2004.

The quotation by James Dobson is from the April 2004 *Focus on the Family Newsletter,* which he read on the radio on March 24, 2004.

Nanette Gartrell and Henny Bos, "U.S. National Longitudinal Lesbian Family Study: Psychological Adjustment of 17-Year-Old Adolescents," *Pediatrics* 126, no. 1 (July 2010), pp. 1–9.

The General Accounting Office (which later became the Government Accountability Office) estimated in 2004 that the Defense of Marriage Act (DOMA) affects the implementation of 1,138 federal laws (source: General Accounting Office, *Defense of Marriage Act: Update to Prior Report,* GAO-04-353R [January 23, 2004]). These laws typically affect employee benefits. Gays who got married under state law are ineligible because DOMA defines marriage as being between a man and a woman, and federal law in America takes precedence over state law.

Gay sex is illegal in 76 countries: see the November 2010 "Harper's Index" in *Harper's Magazine* (source: International Lesbian, Gay, Bisexual, Trans and Intersex Association).

Heather Elise Murphy, *Suicide Risk among Gay, Lesbian, and Bisexual College Youth* (PhD Dissertation, University of Washington, 2007).

Chapter 4: Does Morality Depend on Religion?

77% of Americans support Judge Roy Moore: Gallup Poll, September 2003. 80% of Americans believe in God, and another 12% in a higher power: Gallup Poll, May 2010. 41% believe that Jesus Christ will return to earth by 2050: Pew Research Center for the People & the Press, June 2010. I learned about the clergy's role in assigning movie ratings from the documentary *This Film Is Not Yet Rated* (2006).

The Bertrand Russell quotation is from his essay "A Free Man's Worship," in *Mysticism and Logic* (Garden City, NY: Doubleday, Anchor Books, n.d.), pp. 45–46.

Antony Flew makes the remark about philosophical talent in his *God and Philosophy* (New York: Dell, 1966), p. 109.

Hamlet's exact words were "Why, then 'tis none to you; for there is nothing either good or bad, but thinking makes it so: to me it is a prison" (act 2, scene 2, lines 254–256 of *The Tragedy of Hamlet, Prince of Denmark*, in *The Complete Works of William Shakespeare* [USA: Octopus Books, 1985, p. 844]).

The quotations from Aristotle are from *The Basic Works of Aristotle*, edited by Richard McKeon (New York: Random House, 1941), p. 249, and *The Politics*, translated by T. A. Sinclair (Harmondsworth, Middlesex: Penguin Books, 1962), p. 40.

The quotation from Saint Thomas Aquinas is from the *Summa Theologica*, III *Quodlibet*, 27, translated by Thomas Gilby in *St. Thomas Aquinas: Philosophical Texts* (New York: Oxford University Press, 1960).

The passage supposedly about abortion is Jeremiah 1:4–8. I quoted the "English Standard Version" translation of *The Holy Bible* (2001).

On the history of Catholic thought, see John Connery, SJ, *Abortion: The Development of the Roman Catholic Perspective* (Chicago: Loyola University Press, 1977) (the Church has never said that the fetus acquires a soul at conception: p. 308). I am grateful to Steve Sverdlik for tutoring me in this area.

Pope Benedict XVI's acceptance of evolution and the Big Bang Theory is confirmed by many sources; for example: Lorenzago di Cadore, "Pope: Creation vs. Evolution Clash an 'Absurdity'" (msnbc.

com news services, July 25, 2007), http://www.msnbc.msn.com/id/
19956961/ns/world_news-europe/t/pope-creation-vs-evolution-clash-
absurdity/#.TjoyRb8sU50; and "Pope: God behind Big Bang" (CBS
News, January 7, 2011), http://www.cbsnews.com/8301-501465_
162-20027781-501465.html.

Chapter 5: Ethical Egoism

Each day 22,000 children under five die: *2010 Annual Report*, UNICEF/
United States Fund, p. 1.
    For information about Raoul Wallenberg, see John Bierman,
The Righteous Gentile (New York: Viking Press, 1981). For information
about Gentiles who risked their lives to protect Jews, see http://www
.yadvashem.org.
    The information about Zell Kravinsky comes from "The Gift," an
article by Ian Parker in the *New Yorker* (August 2, 2004). The information about Oseola McCarty comes from Bill Clinton, *Giving: How Each
of Us Can Change the World* (New York: Alfred A. Knopf, 2007), p. 26.
    Dale Carnegie, *How to Win Friends and Influence People* (New York:
Simon and Schuster, 1981; first published in 1936), p. 31.
    The story about Abraham Lincoln is from the Springfield *Moni-
tor,* quoted by Frank Sharp in his *Ethics* (New York: Appleton Century,
1928), p. 75.
    The story about the man who leapt onto the train tracks is from
the January 3, 2007, edition of *The New York Times.*
    The quotations from Ayn Rand are from her book *The Virtue of
Selfishness* (New York: Signet, 1964), pp. 27, 32, 80, and 81.
    The newspaper stories are from *The Baltimore Sun,* August 28, 2001;
The Miami Herald, August 28, 1993, October 6, 1994, and June 2, 1989;
The New York Times, April 28, 2008; and the *Macon Telegraph,* July 15, 2005.
    For Kurt Baier's argument, see his book *The Moral Point of View*
(Ithaca, NY: Cornell University Press, 1958), pp. 189–190.

Chapter 6: The Social Contract Theory

The chapter-opening quote is from chapter 18, section 202, of
Locke's *Second Treatise.* The full sentence reveals a different meaning
than the partial passage: "Wherever law ends, tyranny begins if the
law be transgressed to another's harm."
    Hobbes's estimate of the state of nature is from his *Leviathan,*
Oakeshott edition (Oxford: Blackwell, 1960), chapter 13. See p. 82.

The Rousseau quotation is from *The Social Contract and Discourses*, translated by G. D. H. Cole (New York: Dutton, 1959), pp. 18–19.

That Flood and Dresher first formulated the Prisoner's Dilemma around 1950 is mentioned in Richmond Campbell, "Background for the Uninitiated," *Paradoxes of Rationality and Cooperation*, edited by Richmond Campbell and Lanning Sowden (Vancouver: University of British Columbia Press, 1985), p. 3.

The quotations from King and Waldman may be found in *Civil Disobedience: Theory and Practice*, edited by Hugo Adam Bedau (New York: Pegasus Books, 1967), pp. 76–77, 78, 106, and 107.

The Hume quotation is from "Of the Original Contract," reprinted in *Hume's Moral and Political Philosophy*, edited by Henry D. Aiken (New York: Hafner, 1948), p. 363.

Chapter 7: The Utilitarian Approach

"Priestley was the first (unless it was Beccaria) who taught my lips to pronounce this sacred truth:—That the greatest happiness of the greatest number is the foundation of morals and legislation" (Jeremy Bentham, "Extracts from Bentham's Commonplace Book," *Collected Works*, vol. 10 [Edinburgh: published under the superintendence of John Bowring and printed by William Tait, 1843], p. 142).

Peter Singer says that morality is not a system of nasty puritanical prohibitions in *Practical Ethics*, 2nd ed. (Cambridge: Cambridge University Press, 1993), p. 1.

The account of Freud's death was taken from Ronald W. Clark, *Freud: The Man and the Cause* (New York: Random House, 1980), pp. 525–527; and Paul Ferris, *Dr. Freud: A Life* (Washington, DC: Counterpoint, 1997), pp. 395–397.

The quotations from Bentham are from his book *An Introduction to the Principles of Morals and Legislation*, 1st ed. (printed in 1780; published in 1789), p. 125 (on God) and p. 311 (on animals), available in many reprintings. Bentham discusses sexual ethics in "Offences Against One's Self," written around 1785 and published posthumously.

The quotation from Mill's *On Liberty* (1859) is from paragraph 9 of chap. 1, "Introductory."

Much of the information on marijuana comes from *Pot Politics: Marijuana and the Costs of Prohibition*, edited by Mitch Earleywine (Oxford: Oxford University Press, 2007). The essays cited below are from that book, unless otherwise indicated.

From Mitch Earleywine, "Thinking Clearly about Marijuana Policy," pp. 3–16: One-third of Americans have tried pot (p. 4); on the Gateway Theory (pp. 7–8); when crack is more widely available

(p. 8); the William Bennett quotation (p. 9); marijuana does not cause violence (p. 10). Marijuana does not cause crime: see Eric Blumenson and Eva Nilsen, "Liberty Lost: The Moral Case for Marijuana Law Reform," *Indiana Law Journal* 85 (Winter 2010), pp. 279–300 (p. 284).

In 2007, 5.8% of Americans aged 12 and older had used pot in the past month: "Results from the 2007 National Survey on Drug Use and Health: National Findings," http://oas.samhsa.gov/nsduh/2k7nsduh/2k7results.cfm, p. 1.

Americans spend more than $10 billion per year on marijuana: the Office of National Drug Control Policy's *2008 Marijuana Sourcebook* gives only the old figure that Americans spent $10.5 billion in 2000 (p. 11).

From Robert Gore and Mitch Earleywine, "Marijuana's Perceived Addictiveness: A Survey of Clinicians and Researchers," pp. 176–186: Pot is less addictive than caffeine (p. 179). Gore and Earleywine surveyed 746 drug-abuse counselors, mental health specialists, and academic researchers.

From Wayne Hall, "A Cautious Case for Cannabis Depenalization," pp. 91–112: on driving (p. 92); on the respiratory system (pp. 92–93); on cognitive damage (p. 95); on the Gateway Theory (pp. 96–97); on the difficulties ex-cons face finding jobs (p. 102). Also, according to the Pew Charitable Trusts, the odds of an American rising out of the bottom 20% economic bracket within 20 years depends heavily on whether he is an ex-con: if he is, then the odds are 1 in 50; if he isn't, then the odds are 1 in 7 (*Harper's Magazine*, "Harper's Index," August 2011).

From Kevin A. Sabet, "The (Often Unheard) Case against Marijuana Leniency," pp. 325–352: One joint is like six cigarettes (p. 328, citing the British Lung Foundation from 2002).

From Anthony Liguori, "Marijuana and Driving: Trends, Design Issues, and Future Recommendations," pp. 71–90: See especially p. 83.

From Daniel Egan and Jeffrey A. Miron, "The Budgetary Implications of Marijuana Prohibition," pp. 17–39: on enforcement costs and possible tax gains (p. 29).

Over 700,000 people are arrested each year for possession of marijuana: Blumenson and Nilsen, "Liberty Lost," p. 280. In 2007, there were around 872,720 (total) marijuana arrests: *Crime in the United States, 2007* (Department of Justice/Federal Bureau of Investigation), combining information from the "Persons Arrested" page (http://www.fbi.gov/ucr/cius2007/arrests/index.html) and "Table 29" (http://www.fbi.gov/ucr/cius2007/data/table_29.html). The 44,000+ figure is based on the government's reporting of the number of drug offenders in prison and the percentage of such offenders serving time for marijuana crimes.

Being arrested on marijuana charges is horrible, even if one is not imprisoned: Blumenson and Nilsen, "Liberty Lost," pp. 289–291.

The quotations from Aquinas about animals are from *Summa Contra Gentiles*, book 3, chap. 112. See *Basic Writings of St. Thomas Aquinas*, edited by Anton C. Pegis (New York: Random House, 1945), vol. 2, p. 222.

Richard D. Ryder, "Speciesism in the Laboratory," in *In Defense of Animals: The Second Wave*, edited by Peter Singer (Oxford: Blackwell, 2006). Ryder coined "speciesism": p. ix; the experiments: pp. 91–92.

Chapter 8: The Debate over Utilitarianism

"The utilitarian doctrine is that happiness is desirable . . .": John Stuart Mill, *Utilitarianism* (1861; available in various reprintings), chap. 4, para. 2.

G. E. Moore discusses what has intrinsic value in the last chapter of *Principia Ethica* (Cambridge: Cambridge University Press, 1903).

McCloskey's example of the utilitarian tempted to bear false witness is from his paper "A Non-Utilitarian Approach to Punishment," *Inquiry* 8 (1965), pp. 239–255.

"As strictly impartial as a disinterested and benevolent spectator": John Stuart Mill, *Utilitarianism* (1861; available in various reprintings), chap. 2, para. 18.

The quotation from John Cottingham is from his article "Partialism, Favouritism and Morality," *Philosophical Quarterly* 36 (1986), p. 357.

The Smart quotation is from J. J. C. Smart and Bernard Williams, *Utilitarianism: For and Against* (Cambridge: Cambridge University Press, 1973), p. 68. "Rule worship" is discussed on p. 10.

Frances Howard-Snyder, "Rule Consequentialism Is a Rubber Duck," *American Philosophical Quarterly* 30 (1993), pp. 271–278.

See Gunnar Myrdal, *An American Dilemma: The Negro Problem and American Democracy* (1944; available in various reprintings).

Chapter 9: Are There Absolute Moral Rules?

The quotation from Franklin Roosevelt is from his communication *The President of the United States to the Governments of France, Germany, Italy, Poland and His Britannic Majesty*, September 1, 1939.

The excerpts from Truman's diary are from Robert H. Ferrell, *Off the Record: The Private Papers of Harry S. Truman* (New York: Harper and Row, 1980), pp. 55–56.

The Churchill quote is from Winston S. Churchill, *The Second World War*, vol. 6: *Triumph and Tragedy* (New York: Houghton Mifflin Company, 1953), p. 553.

Anscombe's 1939 pamphlet "The Justice of the Present War Examined," as well as her 1956 pamphlet "Mr Truman's Degree," can be found in G. E. M. Anscombe, *Ethics, Religion and Politics: Collected Philosophical Papers*, vol. 3 (Minneapolis: University of Minnesota Press, 1981). See pp. 64, 65. Also in that volume is her "Modern Moral Philosophy," pp. 26–42 (originally published in *Philosophy* 33, no. 124 [January 1958], pp. 1–19). See p. 27 (critique of Kant) and p. 34 (examples of absolute moral rules).

The grisly details about Hiroshima are from Richard Rhodes, *The Making of the Atomic Bomb* (New York: Simon and Schuster, 1986), p. 715 (birds igniting in midair), and pp. 725–726 (people dying in water).

Kant's statement of the Categorical Imperative is from his *Foundations of the Metaphysics of Morals*, translated by Lewis White Beck (Indianapolis: Bobbs-Merrill, 1959), p. 39.

Kant's "On a Supposed Right to Lie from Altruistic Motives" can be found in *Critique of Practical Reason and Other Writings in Moral Philosophy*, translated by Lewis White Beck (Chicago: University of Chicago Press, 1949). The quotation is from p. 348.

The Peter Geach quotation is from his *God and the Soul* (London: Routledge and Kegan Paul, 1969), p. 128.

MacIntyre's remark is at the beginning of the chapter on Kant in his *A Short History of Ethics* (New York: Macmillan, 1966).

Chapter 10: Kant and Respect for Persons

Kant's remarks on animals are from his *Lectures on Ethics*, translated by Louis Infield (New York: Harper and Row, 1963), pp. 239–240. I altered one sentence without changing its meaning: "he who is cruel to animals also becomes hard in his dealings with men" (not "becomes hard also").

The second formulation of the Categorical Imperative, in terms of treating persons as ends, is in *Foundations of the Metaphysics of Morals*, translated by Lewis White Beck (Indianapolis: Bobbs-Merrill, 1959), p. 47. The remarks about "dignity" and "price" are on p. 53.

Bentham's statement "All punishment is mischief" is from *The Principles of Morals and Legislation* (New York: Hafner, 1948), p. 170.

The quotations from Kant on punishment are from *The Metaphysical Elements of Justice*, translated by John Ladd (Indianapolis: Bobbs-Merrill, 1965), pp. 99–107, except for the quotation about the "right good beating," which is from *Critique of Practical Reason*, translated by Lewis White Beck (Chicago: University of Chicago Press, 1949), p. 170.

On the change in terminology from "prisons" to "correctional facilities," see Blake McKelvey, *American Prisons: A History of Good Intentions* (Montclair, NJ: Patterson Smith, 1977), p. 357.

The United States has about 2.3 million inmates: Bureau of Justice Statistics website, http://bjs.ojp.usdoj.gov/index.cfm?ty= pbdetail&iid=2200. Highest incarceration rate in the world: *Pocket World in Figures, 2011 Edition* (The Economist) (London: Profile Books, 2010), p. 101; and the International Centre for Prison Studies website, http://www.prisonstudies.org/info/worldbrief/wpb_stats.php?area= all&category=wb_poprate. On changes in the American prison system between the 1960s and 1990s, see Eric Schlosser, "The Prison-Industrial Complex," *Atlantic Monthly*, December 1998.

On December 22, 2006, a story on National Public Radio cited California officials as saying that California has the highest recidivism rate in the country.

Jesus talks about "turning the other cheek" in Matthew 5:38–39. I have used the "English Standard Version" translation of *The Holy Bible* (2001).

Chapter 11: Feminism and the Ethics of Care

Heinz's Dilemma is explained in Lawrence Kohlberg, *Essays on Moral Development*, vol. 1: *The Philosophy of Moral Development* (New York: Harper and Row, 1981), p. 12. For the six stages of moral development, see the same work, pp. 409–412.

Amy and Jake are quoted by Carol Gilligan in her *In a Different Voice: Psychological Theory and Women's Development* (Cambridge, MA: Harvard University Press, 1982), pp. 26, 28. The other quotations from Gilligan are from pp. 16–17, 31.

The Virginia Held quotation is from her "Feminist Transformations of Moral Theory," *Philosophy and Phenomenological Research* 50 (1990), p. 344.

Women score higher than men on empathy tests: M. H. Davis, "Measuring Individual Differences in Empathy: Evidence for a Multi-dimensional Approach," *Journal of Personality and Social Psychology* 44, no. 1 (January 1983), pp. 113–126; and P. E. Jose, "The Role of Gender and Gender Role Similarity in Readers' Identification with Story Characters," *Sex Roles* 21, nos. 9–10 (November 1989), pp. 697–713.

Brain scans and punishment: Tania Singer et al., "Empathetic Neural Responses Are Modulated by the Perceived Fairness of Others," *Nature*, January 26, 2006, pp. 466–469.

Roy F. Baumeister, "Is There Anything Good about Men?" American Psychological Association, invited address, 2007 (quotation from p. 9).

Women are only slightly more care-oriented than men: Sara Jaffee and Janet Shibley Hyde, "Gender Differences in Moral Orientation: A Meta-Analysis," *Psychological Bulletin* 126, no. 5 (2000), pp. 703–726.

Male/female differences appear at an early age: Larry Cahill, "His Brain, Her Brain," *Scientific American*, April 25, 2005 (8 pages), citing the work of Simon Baron-Cohen and Svetlana Lutchmaya.

"'Care' is the new buzzword": Annette Baier, *Moral Prejudices* (Cambridge, MA: Harvard University Press, 1994), p. 19. The other quotations from Baier are from p. 4 ("connect their ethics of love") and p. 2 ("honorary women").

The figures about HIV are from *Global Report: UNAIDS Report on the Global AIDS Epidemic/2010:* 2.5 million children have HIV (p. 23); around one-fourth get decent medical care (pp. 97–98); around half of pregnant women are protecting their children (p. 78).

The quotations from Nel Noddings are from her book *Caring: A Feminine Approach to Ethics and Moral Education* (Berkeley: University of California Press, 1984), pp. 149–155.

Chapter 12: Virtue Ethics

The quotations from Aristotle are from book 2 of the *Nicomachean Ethics,* translated by Martin Ostwald (Indianapolis: Bobbs-Merrill, 1962), except for the quotation about friendship, which is from book 8, and the quotation about visiting foreign lands, which is Martha C. Nussbaum's translation in her article "Non-Relative Virtues: An Aristotelian Approach," in *Midwest Studies in Philosophy,* vol. 13: *Ethical Theory: Character and Virtue,* edited by Peter A. French, Theodore E. Uehling Jr., and Howard K. Wettstein (Notre Dame, IN: University of Notre Dame Press, 1988), pp. 32–53.

Pincoffs's suggestion about the nature of virtue appears in his book *Quandaries and Virtues: Against Reductivism in Ethics* (Lawrence: University of Kansas Press, 1986), p. 78.

Peter Geach's remark about courage is from his book *The Virtues* (Cambridge: Cambridge University Press, 1977), p. xxx. The story about Saint Athanasius is on p. 114.

Jesus says that we should give all we have to help the poor in Matthew 19:21–24, Mark 10:21–25, and Luke 18:22–25.

Plato's *Euthyphro* is available in several translations, including Hugh Tredennick and Harold Tarrant's in *Plato: The Last Days of Socrates* (New York: Penguin Books, 2003).

The Nietzsche quotation is from *Twilight of the Idols,* "Morality as Anti-Nature," pt. 6, translated by Walter Kaufmann in *The Portable Nietzsche* (New York: Viking Press, 1954), p. 491.

Michael Stocker's example is from his article "The Schizophrenia of Modern Ethical Theories," *Journal of Philosophy* 73 (1976), pp. 453–466.

The John Stuart Mill quote is from chapter 2 of his *Utilitarianism* (1861; available in various reprintings).

Elizabeth Anscombe rejects the notion of "morally right" in her article "Modern Moral Philosophy," *Philosophy* 33 (1958), pp. 1–19, reprinted in *Ethics, Religion and Politics: The Collected Philosophical Papers of G. E. M. Anscombe,* vol. 3 (Minneapolis: University of Minnesota Press, 1981), pp. 26–42 ("it would be a great improvement": p. 33).

Chapter 13: What Would a Satisfactory Moral Theory Be Like?

The age of the universe is taken from the "WMAP" data as presented on NASA's website. "WMAP" is the Wilkinson Microwave Anisotropy Probe, which was launched in 2001 and collected data until 2010.

The Sidgwick quotation is from Henry Sidgwick, *The Methods of Ethics,* 7th ed. (London: Macmillan, 1907), p. 413.

One-fifth of children miss their vaccinations, resulting in two million annual deaths: *2010 Annual Report,* UNICEF/United States Fund, p. 15.

John Rawls discusses the "natural lottery" on p. 74 of *A Theory of Justice* (Cambridge, MA: Harvard University Press, 1971), and on p. 64 of the revised edition of that book, published in 1999.

Index